The Counsellor's Handbook

The Counsellor's Handbook

A practical A–Z guide to professional and clinical practice

Rowan Bayne, Ian Horton, Tony Merry
and Elizabeth Noyes
Psychology Department
University of East London
London
UK

CHAPMAN & HALL

London · Glasgow · Weinheim · New York · Tokyo · Melbourne · Madras

Published by Chapman & Hall, 2–6 Boundary Row,
London SE1 8HN, UK

Chapman & Hall, 2–6 Boundary Row, London SE1 8HN, UK

Blackie Academic & Professional, Wester Cleddens Road,
Bishopbriggs, Glasgow G64 2NZ, UK

Chapman & Hall, GmbH, Pappelallee 3, 69469 Weinheim, Germany

Chapman & Hall Inc., One Penn Plaza, 41st Floor, New York
NY 10119, USA

Chapman & Hall Japan, Thomson Publishing Japan, Hirakawacho
Nemoto Building, 6F, 1–7–11 Hirakawa-cho, Chiyoda-ku, Tokyo 102,
Japan

Chapman & Hall Australia, Thomas Nelson Australia, 102 Dodds
Street, South Melbourne, Victoria 3205, Australia

Chapman & Hall India, R. Seshadri, 32 Second Main Road, CIT East,
Madras 600 035, India

Distributed in the USA and Canada by Singular Publishing Group Inc.,
4284 41st Street, San Diego, California 92105

First edition 1994

© 1994 Rowan Bayne, Ian Horton, Tony Merry and Elizabeth Noyes

Typeset in 10/12 Palatino by Mews Photosetting, Beckenham, Kent
Printed in Great Britain by Page Bros (Norwich) Ltd

ISBN 0 412 55220 5   1 56593 293 5 (USA)

A catalogue record for this book is available from the British Library

Library of Congress Catalog Card Number: 94-70923

∞ Printed on permanent acid-free text paper, manufactured in
accordance with ANSI/NISO Z39.48-1992 and ANSI/NISO Z39.48-1984
(Permanence of paper).

Contents

CONTENTS xi

Acknowledgements

We would like to thank all the people who have contributed to this book, particularly Susamma Ajith and Ann Stapleton for their skill with word-processing and for calmly making time in a busy office, and Rosemary Morris, our commissioning editor, for her quiet persistence and clear sense of boundaries. The book is dedicated to the wonderfully varied students, past and present, on our Diploma in Counselling courses.

Introduction

This book is for counsellors and trainee counsellors. It offers ideas, evidence, arguments, information and occasionally advice on day-to-day aspects of counselling. We think of these as in three broad categories:

- Apparently peripheral aspects, like fees, furniture, holidays and smoking. Many books on counselling either ignore these or only mention them in passing. We treat them as important in their own right because they make effective counselling less likely if they are neglected, and because counsellors sometimes worry about them.
- Generic aspects, like boundaries, collusion, emotions and empathy. By 'generic' we mean not specific to a particular approach to counselling. For example, paraphrasing is a general skill (and included) while 'splitting' is specific to a particular approach (and not included).

- Issues on which there is marked variation in practice, e.g. assessment, psychodiagnosis. For these we outline the main options and arguments.

In this introduction we would like to say something about three things: how we see the book being useful; its content; and the terms 'counselling' and 'psychotherapy'.

USING THIS BOOK

We want counsellors with a pressing query or a vague disquiet to find ideas that stimulate, crystallize, challenge or support their own theories, values and feelings without having to read lots of other material (irrelevant to the particular concern) first. The book is therefore organized alphabetically, with the entries as their own index, so that everything we've written on a particular topic can be found and read very quickly. Further reading – longer discussions, research papers – is suggested for follow-up if desired. We hope too that the book will be enjoyed in more leisurely, less-pressured moods, but essentially it is a concise discussion of central, non-partisan elements of counselling with, where appropriate, practical guidelines.

CONTENT OF THE BOOK

The nature of our book can also be defined by comparing it with other books. Four recent books seem particularly relevant in this respect. *An A–Z of Counselling Theory and Practice* (Stewart, 1992) presents an overview of the main approaches and skills of counselling, but the overlap in headings between this book and ours is only about 5% because Stewart tries to encompass all of counselling and we have chosen to focus on the three aspects indicated above. Similarly, Feltham and Dryden's (1993) *Dictionary of Counselling* contains concise definitions of more than 1100 terms, while we discuss about 150.

The other two books are much closer to ours, in different ways. First, *Brief Counselling: A Practical Guide for Beginners* (Dryden and Feltham, 1992) shares the same general aim as this book: to help counsellors examine and improve their counselling. However, Dryden and Feltham take a more leisurely tour through a specific approach to brief counselling, beginning with orientation and assessment, then change, the middle phase, and ending, while we focus more sharply on particular elements of counselling and take a cross-sectional rather than a sequential view.

Second, in *Questions and Answers on Psychology in Action* (Dryden, 1993), several authors discuss 30 questions about counselling and counsellor training. Although there is more overlap, in content and style, between this book and ours, and the emphasis in both books is on application, the differences are again substantial and we discuss a wider range of topics more briefly. Some examples of the questions and topics discussed in Dryden (1993) but not by us are: Using hypnosis in counselling; Who should trainee counsellors counsel?; Spirituality and the counsellor; and Does being a psychologist help a counsellor in his or her work?

Finally, our experience and training, though diverse, hardly reflects the whole of counselling, and your favourite or most puzzling (and fairly general) concept or query may therefore be missing. If it is, please tell us. We would welcome comments on what we might have included, and on other aspects of the book. Our address is: Psychology Department, UEL, The Green, London E15 4LZ, UK.

COUNSELLING AND PSYCHOTHERAPY

There often seems to be a difference between counselling and psychotherapy, but so far no one has been able to define with sufficient clarity what it is. In BAC's words: 'It is not possible to make a generally accepted distinction between counselling and psychotherapy. There are well-founded traditions which use the terms interchangeably and others which distinguish them'

(1990a, 3.3). Thorne (1992) remarks on how 'disarming' these statements are, and how different reality is. He deals briskly with the distinctions which have been put forward, and with the 'dismal quest' for them. Rather, he hopes for a British Association for Counselling and Psychotherapy, based on the common elements in all approaches. We will use the two terms – and counsellor/psychotherapist/therapist interchangeably.

A

ABUSE (*See also*: Anger, Empathy, Boundaries, Collusion, Counselling, Post-Traumatic Stress Disorder, Power, Sexual attraction, Touch)

Counselling the survivors of emotional, physical or sexual abuse requires great sensitivity. Both establishing trust and exploration need to proceed at the client's own, often painfully slow, pace. Moreover, sometimes a large amount of previously unexpressed material pours out. Collusion of silence can be a hazard in this type of counselling; it is tempting to let clients avoid the painful expression of their past experience. Shillito-Clarke (1993) recommends the accounts in Walker (1992a) as a way of exploring reactions: 'I found it difficult to read without pausing between accounts or resorting to defensive strategies. In this respect, the book may prove an interesting testing ground for anyone interested in, but unsure of their ability to work with, survivors' (p. 219).

Survivors of abuse sometimes suppress their emotions and memories to the point of forgetting about them altogether. In the USA, people with recently unearthed memories of sexual abuse have sued the alleged abusers for events that happened 20 or even 40 years earlier. Loftus (1993) discusses some of the problematic issues raised:

1. How common is it for memories of child abuse to be repressed?
2. How are jurors and judges likely to react to claims of repressed memories?
3. What are the memories like?
4. How authentic are they?

A major problem is that remembering things is a creative process: we simplify, shape and distort our memories, create false memories, and often forget significant events quite soon after they've happened (e.g. Loftus and Loftus, 1980). Studies of counsellors and therapists whose clients report previously repressed memories conclude that the memories are seen as authentic because of accompanying symptoms, 'body memories' such as a rash matching injuries, emotional pain and occasionally corroborating evidence from others (Loftus, 1993, p. 523). Moreover, there are cases in which people were led to believe – by a therapist or therapy group – that they were abused and later reinterpreted these 'memories' as false.

Two practical implications for counsellors are to raise the possibility of abuse either with great care, or not at all, and that using hypnosis or fantasy exercises to encourage memory is dangerous: they are more likely to increase confidence in what is recalled than its accuracy, however good the intentions of the counsellor or therapist. There are obvious costs, for the alleged survivors as well as those accused, of uncritically accepting false memories as facts.

Draucker's (1992) book integrates ideas, practice and research on sexual abuse, and much of it is relevant to emotional and physical abuse and to counselling in general.

ACCENTING (*See also*: Concreteness, Empathy, Paraphrasing, Questions, Silence)

Accenting is the skill of saying back one or two words to help your client clarify or explore more deeply, e.g. client: 'I was fairly happy about that . . .' Counsellor: 'Fairly happy'. It is best used sparingly.

ACCEPTANCE, *See* Respect

ACCREDITATION, OF INDIVIDUAL COUNSELLORS BY BAC (*See also***:** Professional development, Professionalism, Recognition, of counsellor training/education courses, Supervision)

An accredited counsellor is now commonly taken to be someone who has gained accreditation through the scheme introduced by the British Association for Counselling (BAC) in 1983. It is a form of peer appraisal for generic counsellors, based on 900 hours of training and practice. The 900 hours includes 250 hours' theory, 200 hours' skills development and case discussion and 450 hours of supervised work with clients over a minimum period of 3 years. Evidence is required of serious and continuing commitment to professional and personal development, to consultation or supervision and to continuing in supervision for the period of accreditation. The scheme is open to current members of BAC who assent to the BAC Code of Ethics. Applications, which include case studies, a statement of counselling philosophy, and supervisor's and referee's reports are judged without any face-to-face meeting. Counsellors who have successfully completed a BAC-recognized course have an easier task in that they complete only one case study and do not have to provide any training details.

Once accredited, the counsellor is required to maintain not less than 150 hours' counselling each year and not less than 1½ hours' supervision each month, an approximate ratio of 1:9

supervision to counselling hours. Unlike practice in other professional areas, e.g. social work and nursing, accreditation is for a 5-year period only, after which counsellors need to re-apply and demonstrate their competence anew.

While the scheme was originally intended to protect the interests of the consumer, it is now used by many counsellors as a way of achieving professional status and is sometimes seen as an informal 'licence to practise'. It is a voluntary not a statutory scheme, but registration is currently being discussed.

Granting of professional status usually depends on some form of certification by a professional body. However, the scheme is not without its critics/controversy, and many individual members are not eligible to apply as they are people using counselling skills at work rather than counsellors as defined by BAC. The effort of applying and the anxiety and potential embarrassment of being rejected are obvious disincentives for others. For some counsellors, any authorization system with its unavoidable judgemental element, and the trend towards professionalization, are anathema.

The scheme is now widely respected, with employers frequently asking for BAC-accredited counsellors or at least eligibility for accreditation. An external review (Foss, 1986) recommended that the scheme become more rigorous and that separate schemes be developed for accreditation of supervision and training courses. These have now been introduced.

ACTIVE LISTENING, *See* Accenting, Empathy, Paraphrasing, Questions, Silence, Summarizing

ADVERTISING (*See also*: Codes of ethics, Marketing)

In some professions, medicine for example, advertising of services is illegal. In counselling, it is both legal and professionally acceptable to advertise as long as you do not state or imply that you can cure people of any sickness, ill-health or disturbance. You can say that you can help with these problems and others like them, but you should not claim to be in possession of special knowledge or skills that guarantee any form of success. The British Code of Advertising practice (8th edition, 1988), is available free from the Advertising Standards Authority, Brook House, 2–16 Torrington Place, London WC1E 7HN (071-580 5555). It requires advertisements to be 'legal', decent, honest and truthful, and also contains a clause stating that failure to substantiate any claims made, and to do so quickly, itself contravenes the Code.

It is advisable, therefore, to restrict your advertising to straightforward statements of any areas you specialize in (such as stress or depression), the approach you use, and how potential clients can contact you. The costs of advertising can be claimed against tax, providing they are 'wholly and exclusively' incurred for the purpose of business.

Some counsellors advertise in their local press, in specialist magazines, in meeting places such as doctors' surgeries (provided permission has been obtained from the doctors concerned), and drop-in and day centres. The BAC publishes an Annual Directory of Counsellors and Psychotherapists (which includes accredited and non-accredited members of BAC), and this is a good way to get yourself known, but there can be an up to 12 months' wait between providing BAC with your details, and their publication in the next directory. Local BAC branches also produce directories of counsellors.

If you produce any promotional literature (handouts, leaflets), again be sure not to make claims that imply any guarantee of success. The BAC Code of Ethics states that when announcing counselling services, counsellors should limit the information they give to name, address, telephone number, hours available, relevant qualifications, and a brief listing of the services offered. Care should also be taken not to indicate affiliation with an organization in a manner which falsely implies accreditation, validation or sponsorship by that organization.

ADVICE GIVING (*See also***:** Challenging, Counselling, Empathy, Frame of reference, Guidance, Information, Sued (being))

A basic aim of counselling is to support clients in taking responsibility for their decisions and in being more independent. Generally, advice from you is inconsistent with this aim, and many counsellors therefore do not give advice. *Not* giving advice can be

therapeutic in itself: it 'says', in effect, 'When you've explored what's troubling you, you'll see it more clearly and know what to do'. Lazarus offers a radically different view: 'I will often be fairly free with my advice', though he adds that he always phrases it 'This is the way I see it' (in Dryden, 1991, p. 60).

AGGRESSIVE AND VIOLENT CLIENTS, *See* Anger, Violence and its prevention

ANGER, EXPRESSION OF (*See also*: Emotions, Empathy, Journal)

Expression of anger is often encouraged in counselling, on the grounds that (i) suppressed emotions cause problems which are helped by the releasing of anger and/or (ii) that experiences are more likely to be understood and assimilated if spoken about, and that experiencing emotions facilitates this process. Some approaches, notably psychodynamic, see expression as vitally important. Others see anger as a manifestation of depression, or as an expression of fear, with fear as the emotion really needing to be expressed.

In contrast, research on anger suggests that expressing it is usually unhelpful, and that the question of whether or not a person should express or suppress anger is better put as: when does a person benefit? What kind of person? And, more subtly, 'When should an individual neither express anger nor suppress it, but stop generating the emotion in the first place? Why does the same action (say, talking about one's anger) produce a feeling of communication in one circumstance and the opposite feeling in another?' (Tavris, 1984, p. 172).

Tavris' general conclusion about expressing anger is that just 'releasing it' tends to consolidate the anger, exclude other emotions and make other people angrier too (1984, 1989). Anger can be expressed constructively, especially perhaps in counselling, but the view that not expressing it is stressful and that releasing it is healthy in a 'cathartic' way is too simple.

There are many ways of helping clients become more aware of their anger: empathy; experiential exercises (e.g. Ernst and Goodison, 1982); holding a conversation with it (How long have you been there? What do you want?); drawing it; writing to it. Sometimes more physical approaches, like punching cushions, allow a non-verbal release of emotion and clearer understanding.

ANGER, COPING WITH (*See also*: Codes of ethics, Confidentiality, Emotions, Empathy, Ethical analysis, Experiments, Office, Sued (being), Touch, Violence and its prevention)

Some clients are so angry that you may feel, or be, threatened. In such cases empathy and – when your client is calm – an 'anger management' approach may be helpful. Novaco (1975) uses cognitive and behavioural techniques to help clients become aware of their arousal and of the thought patterns which lead to angry outbursts.

By relaxing and learning to reconstrue those thoughts, the client may be helped to work towards more manageable behaviour.

A contract establishing the difference between 'feeling angry' and 'aggressive behaviour' (and agreeing not to behave aggressively during counselling), can clarify the situation and increase confidence. However, the inclusion of details on what will happen if the client gets violent may either be useful or reduce trust, depending on the situation. All clients require recognition of their anger and a chance to talk about it, though for some the thought of talking about it is too threatening. It needs to be made explicit that *clients* can decide what is right for them. Then they are more in control and less likely to feel threatened or to resort to violence.

How you respond to a potentially violent client if she or he gets upset also needs to be established early on. Touch is risky and in some areas and cultures an aggressive person tends to see prolonged looking as 'eye-balling' and may respond accordingly; in others, *not* looking can be seen as furtive and cause unease and aggression. Comfortable 'personal space' also varies from person to person and culture to culture. You can be clear about these factors and agree that the client will take deep breaths and (literally) 'count to 10', or focus her or his attention 'out', e.g. by looking for all the things of a particular colour in the room. These strategies aid self-control but a balance between self-control and clarifying emotions needs to be kept in mind.

ANGER, IN COUNSELLORS (*See also*: Immediacy, Self-disclosure, Stress, Supervision)

Faced, in the session itself, with their own anger, counsellors are sometimes in a dilemma about whether to talk about it then or later. In other words, do you use the skills of self-disclosure or immediacy in the session, or wait until supervision? There is no easy answer; it depends on the circumstances. The first consideration is whether or not disclosing your anger will help your client. This is not as straightforward as it seems; what you might see as being helpful to clients in that you are letting them know their effect on people, they might see as unempathic, and the counselling could be disrupted. If in any doubt, it is better to discuss your angry response in supervision. There you can clarify whether you are picking up on your client's anger, or if it is your own anger which is being stimulated. It is then possible to examine how you could enable your client to get in touch with her or his own anger, while you talk about your feelings with your own counsellor.

ANSWERPHONE (*See also*: Nuisance telephone calls)

Answering machines can make it easier for people to contact each other (and to avoid contact!), but they are very off-putting for some people, perhaps especially for those who may be nervous about making contact with you in the first place. The message you leave can make all the difference.

We suggest saying when you will be available, if this is possible, and that giving your name is more friendly than a number (though some people may prefer not to take this risk). So a possible message is: 'Hello, this is John Smith. I'm unable to take your call at the moment. I'm usually available to answer the phone between ten and eleven each weekday morning, but if you'd prefer, please leave your name and a telephone number after the tone, and I will call you as soon as I can.' It is better not to say 'There is no-one here at the moment'. It may help a burglar.

ANXIETY (*See also*: Depression, Emotions, Stress)

Although some anxiety is overt, it can also underly depression, obsessions, hysteria, bodily symptoms and phobias. Counselling aims to help clients face up to anxiety, through, for example, empathy, restructuring of thoughts, facing 'existential givens', or physically facing whatever is anxiety-provoking. There is no clear evidence that one method is better than another, but some clients may prefer a particular approach. It may be helpful to give a choice as part of the process of encouraging clients to take responsibility e.g. do they want to look at thoughts, feelings, or actions, or any combination of the three? The more extreme the anxiety the more likely it is that a variety of approaches need to be used in its management. See Hallam (1991) and van Deurzen Smith (1990).

APPROPRIATENESS OF COUN-SELLING, *See* Assessment, Contra-indications, Referral

ASSERTIVENESS (*See also*: Self-awareness, Thoughts, Values)

Assertiveness can be defined as 'being able to express and act on your rights as a person while respecting the same rights in others'. Three other levels of definition are in terms of the rights themselves, styles of behaviour and skills. Rakos (1991) reviews a variety of definitions (one author discusses 20) and the problems associated with them. He draws attention to the distinction between assertiveness **therapy** (a more remedial approach, in clinical settings) and assertiveness **training** (for professional groups and the general public) (p. 187). Assertiveness training is for people who are already relatively assertive but who wish to develop particular skills and qualities further. Assertiveness therapy is 'a treatment of choice for most people with interpersonal difficulties' (Corey, 1991, p. 305).

The terms used by Dickson (1987) for styles of behaviour which are *not* assertive are fairly standard: aggressive, passive and manipulative (indirectly aggressive). Lists of assertive

Table 1 Assertive rights

1. I have the right to be treated with respect	**and**	Others have the right to be treated with respect.
2. I have the right to express my thoughts, opinions and values	**and**	Others have the right to express their thoughts, opinions and values.
3. I have the right to express my feelings	**and**	Others have the right to express their feelings.
4. I have the right to say 'No' without feeling guilty	**and**	Others have the right to say 'No' without feeling guilty.
5. I have the right to be successful	**and**	Others have the right to be successful.
6. I have the right to make mistakes	**and**	Others have the right to make mistakes.
7. I have the right to change my mind	**and**	Others have the right to change their minds.
8. I have the right to say that I don't understand	**and**	Others have the right to say that they don't understand.
9. I have the right to ask for what I want	**and**	Others have the right to ask for what they want.
10. I have the right to decide for myself whether or not I am responsible for another person's problem	**and**	Others have the right to decide for themselves whether or not they are responsible for another person's problem.
11. I have the right to choose not to assert myself	**and**	Others have the right to choose not to assert themselves.

rights vary more than the styles, but the left hand column of Table 1 is representative. Its format, taken from Bond (1986), is unusual though and makes the 'respect for others' element in assertiveness explicit.

Different writers offer different ideas about the skills of assertiveness, but 'saying no' and 'making requests' are basic. Saying no includes the key skill – strongly supported by research (Rakos, 1991) – of 'empathic assertion'. Other assertive skills are giving and receiving compliments, and giving and receiving criticism. Dickson (1987) is a practical source, and for both sexes despite its title.

CULTURAL BIAS AND ASSERTIVE-NESS (See also: Multiculturalism, Self-awareness)

An issue in training and therapy, expressed as a critical (even hostile) question, is; 'What is "assertive" in one culture is not in another: how do you deal with that? Isn't assertiveness training just another attempt to impose middle-class, white values, attitudes and norms of behaviour on ethnic minorities and on the working-class?' This criticism is hard to maintain. First, some white middle-class values are antagonistic to assertiveness, e.g. that women should defer to men and men shouldn't cry. Second, assertiveness is explicit about its values. However, some of the values do clash with those of some cultures and other groups. For example, subservience and self-sacrifice are highly valued in some groups, and social contexts vary in their openness to change and

development in their members (Bimrose, 1993).

Rakos' (1991) solution to the problem of cultural bias is 'bicultural competence' (e.g. p. 89). By this he means the particular group practising assertive skills for both the 'mainstream' culture and, where applicable, their own subculture and/or the subculture of people they work with. Another solution is to emphasize individual style and self-awareness. Assertiveness training is then seen more as consciousness-raising to allow greater choice, including whether or not to use skills to challenge a particular social context, than as prescribing how or when to use the skills.

ASSESSMENT (See also: Beginnings, Contract, Contraindications, Psychodiagnosis, Referral)

Counsellors vary radically in their attitudes towards assessment. Some counsellors use a range of assessment procedures which may involve lengthy intake interviews or case histories and diagnostic classification systems (e.g. DSM-III). For others, the whole idea of assessment is anathema. They regard it as something 'done to the client', synonymous with the medical model of diagnosis, prescription and treatment in which the balance of power, responsibility and role of expert is held by the counsellor. While many counsellors prefer not to use any type of formal procedures and may avoid using the term 'assessment', few would argue with the need to obtain some information when starting work with each client.

Whatever your theoretical orientation, assessment will typically be concerned with one or more of the following objectives:

1. To help you and your client understand the nature of the client's presenting problem and related issues.
2. To identify the factors that may be associated with the problem and the client's experience or behaviour.
3. To determine the client's expectations and desired outcomes.
4. To collect baseline data that can be compared with subsequent data to evaluate progress.
5. To facilitate the client's learning and motivation by sharing the counsellor's view of the problem. This may in itself contribute to therapeutic change through increasing self-awareness.
6. To produce an initial assessment (formulation) which provides the counsellor with the basis for, first, making a decision about whether to offer a counselling contract, to initiate referral or to suggest that counselling would not be appropriate, and second to provide the basis for developing a therapeutic or counselling plan, including the length and pattern of contract.

CATEGORIES IN ASSESSMENT

Various kinds of information can be gathered or areas explored during assessment:

1. Presenting problem – including affective (emotions, feelings, mood), somatic (body-related sensations), behavioural (what the client does or doesn't do) and cognitive (thoughts, beliefs, attitudes, values, images, fantasies, internal dialogue) elements.
2. Antecedents – factors that may have influenced or caused the presenting problem.
3. Consequences – factors which may be maintaining it, at least in part.
4. Previous attempts to solve or cope with it.
5. Client resources and strengths.
6. The frequency, duration and severity of the problem, i.e. how long or how often the problem occurs, when it first started and its effects.

ASSESSMENT FORMULATION (*See also*: Contract, Expectations, History, Information, Psychodiagnosis, Referral)

An assessment formulation is an attempt to construct a picture of what is going on within the client and to describe and offer some explanation of the presenting problem. It may include some tentative ideas about emerging themes or possible connections between the client's past and present behaviour and experience. Depending on your theoretical orientation, the formulation may hypothesize about the possible origin and development of the problem and why it persists.

The formulation integrates information from a variety of sources:

1. The client's account of the experience.
2. The client's developmental history and social context.
3. Your experience of the client.
4. Your own theoretical frameworks.

These sources may be supplemented by such techniques as:

● client diaries about the problem;
● genograms, life-space diagrams;
● psychological tests;
● DSM-III classifications.

AVOIDANCE, BY CLIENTS (*See also*: Boredom, Challenge, Denial, Empathy, Immediacy, Referral, Reluctant clients)

Sometimes clients avoid topics which they consciously do not want to talk about. When they do not say that they are doing this and just avoid the topics, it can make counselling difficult and frustrating. This problem may be overcome by agreeing (in the contract) that if there is an area the client wishes not to talk about, then they make this clear and the counsellor respects their wish. Once clients realize that their wishes have been respected and that they can trust the counsellor, they are able to relax and usually quite quickly are able to talk about the area they were originally avoiding; however, we do *not* recommend expecting this outcome, or using the agreement as a manipulative technique.

When clients are unaware that they are avoiding, it might be for some general reason, like finding it difficult to talk about emotions and feelings; or they might be suppressing a specific event. Usually, counselling

will gradually (at the client's pace) encourage more openness, but for very deeply suppressed fears it may take many months. One form of avoidance is for the client to talk about everybody and everything but themselves. Often a good empathic statement is the best strategy, e.g. 'You were upset by your parents' behaviour' could bring a client back to themselves after complaining about their parents (Egan, 1990).

AVOIDANCE, BY COUNSELLORS (*See also*: Collusion, Contract, Emotions, Empathy, Feelings, Paraphrasing, Questions, Self-awareness)

It is easy to collude with a client's wish to avoid a subject, especially if it is a difficult subject for the counsellor too. Each time the client approaches it the counsellor may focus on a safer topic or ask an unnecessary question, so encouraging the client to continue avoiding. The question 'what are you feeling?', which is intended to help clients look deeper at themselves, is often unhelpful here, for the following reasons:

1. It is a question, which tends to make clients think. They may therefore answer in terms of thoughts, rather than emotions, images or feelings.
2. It is asked by the counsellor in desperation as they have not managed to pick up the emotions or feelings stated or implied by the client. Thus the client's real feelings have been ignored, which reinforces avoidance.

3. It might push the client towards a feeling which is very frightening and which they are not ready to face. They then become even more likely to avoid. In all these cases, an empathic response is likely to achieve more.

To avoid avoidance the counsellor needs to be self-aware, probably as a result of good training and personal counselling. Regular supervision also helps spot any collusion with client avoidance. A general academic text is Edelstein *et al.* (1989) and a more specific one, Hayes and Melancon (1989).

B

BEGINNINGS (*See also*: Assessment, Codes of ethics, Confidentiality, Contract, Duration, Expectations, Fees, Frequency, Information, Questions, Rapport, Referral, Working alliance)

The beginning can be crucial. Some clients are optimistic and ready to work hard, others are very anxious about counselling (Pipes *et al.*, 1985). This is not surprising: they are putting themselves in the hands of a stranger at a point in their life when they feel vulnerable, and when they may have limited or inaccurate knowledge about counselling.

From the counsellor's point of view, beginning work with clients involves both content and process: helping your clients explore what is troubling them and also establishing a relationship. Different counsellors and approaches to counselling place more or less emphasis on each of the following:

1. **Role induction**. This includes helping your clients explore any fears, fantasies and expectations, in particular how long counselling might last and what will happen in the sessions. You may find it helpful to prepare a brief account of your own view of counselling. What seems most important is that you and your clients work towards and negotiate a common understanding of what is involved.

2. **Establishing rapport** (sometimes called 'the therapeutic alliance' or the 'working alliance').

3. **Information-gathering**. This is about encouraging your clients to talk openly about themselves and their problems. Other possible topics are the 'trigger' – why they came to counselling at this point – and previous experience of counselling.

4. **Assessment**.

5. **Practical agreements** about times and days to meet, etc.

BELIEFS, IRRATIONAL, *See* Thoughts

'BLOCKED' CLIENTS, *See* Avoidance, Challenge, Referral, Reluctant clients

BOOKS, SELF-HELP

Rosen (1981, 1987) attacked the untested materials and exaggerated claims of most self-help books and tapes. He was scathing about titles that encourage unrealistic expectations, e.g. *Winning the Losing Battle: Why I will Never be Fat Again, Understanding People,* or *How to Be Your Very Own Shrink,* and *Spare the Couch: Self-Change for Self-Improvement.* And he suggested some guidelines for evaluating how helpful or not a self-help book or tape is likely to be (Rosen, 1981). The guidelines, expressed more simply and combined with those of Webb (1981), included:

1. Does the book claim or promise too much?
2. Does the book specify its limitations?
3. Is the advice specific or vague?
4. Is there a warning about placebo effects?
5. Does the book include or cite sound evidence of effectiveness? i.e. more than opinions, anecdotes and testimonials.
6. Are there criteria for evaluating progress?

While these suggestions seem appropriately rigorous, others are more arguable, e.g. 'Is the author appropriately qualified? and 'Has the *book itself* (rather than the techniques) been tested for effectiveness?'. The first could be seen as self-interest on the part of psychologists, and irrelevant if the other criteria are met. In support of the second, Rosen cited studies showing that techniques which work with 'minimal therapist assistance' do not work or work much less well without it. Indeed, some self-help programmes have been shown to make a problem worse. On the other hand, when effectiveness is unknown, and appropriate guidelines for use are given, it seems reasonable to suggest things to try. Rosen's criteria are firmly within an empirical framework, when often in counselling and self-help the research has not yet been done, or is inconclusive. At the same time, where research has been done and seems sound, then it would be unethical and unprofessional to ignore it.

BOREDOM (*See also*: Challenge, Confrontation, Congruence, Immediacy, Intuition, Process, Self-awareness)

When you feel bored in a counselling session, it is usually better not to be stoical about it. One strategy is to focus on the client's non-verbal behaviour, another to 'change gear' into a free-flowing attention and see what comes to mind. A third possibility was suggested by Rogers: to say in a positive and constructive way that you are bored and that you want to find out what's going on. This strategy is not itself boring.

A fourth possibility is to be more concrete. Yalom (1989, pp. 95–99) discusses in detail his decision to confront Betty about boredom as the outstanding characteristic of his experience of their relationship, and how he proceeded. He clarified how much of the boredom was his problem, and identified two characteristics of Betty that were boring: she did not reveal anything intimate about herself and her 'forced gaiety'. Then he chose to confront her, first about how much she revealed, and later with her being 'jolly' and 'entertaining'. A principle which Yalom (1989) draws on is that 'if something big in a relationship is not being talked about . . . then nothing else of importance will be discussed either (p. 114). Other principles to consider are trying hunches much earlier, and to do something about persistent emotions.

BOUNDARIES (*See also*: Abuse, Assertiveness, 'Burnout', Confidentiality, Contract, Drama triangle, Endings, Friendship, Power, Privacy, Sexual attraction, Stress, Supervision, Time boundaries)

Boundaries are a part of being clear with yourself and with clients, and being trustworthy. They offer stability, and apply the idea (and existential fact) that there are limits to relationships, including the counselling relationship. However, counsellors do sometimes become too involved and want to give more and more to clients, or to a particular client. This is counterproductive for everyone, including other clients. Stressed or 'burned out' counsellors are less likely to be effective. Relevant boundaries include those of time, space (privacy), confidentiality, structure of the session, and overall structure, and those between counsellors and clients, and thoughts and emotions.

Walker (1992b, pp. 126–29) discusses the boundary of availability, under the heading 'Ring me whenever you need to'. She acted 'with good intentions but poor judgment' with a particularly distressed client, by offering to be available between sessions. It is not that this was undesirable in itself but that it was ill-considered at the time, and reflected her own needs and anxieties. It also did not help the client.

BRAINSTORMING (*See also*: Counselling, Freewriting, Power, Values)

Brainstorming is a standard element in setting goals and planning action. Once your clients are sufficiently clear about a problem, the next step is for them to decide what, if anything, to do about it, and the idea of brainstorming is simply generating and usually writing down lots of ideas in a free-wheeling way, without judging or censoring them at all, and going for quantity, including what may seem absurd ideas. The next step is to try combining and grouping the ideas, and finally, to evaluate them.

BRIEF COUNSELLING (*See also*: Contract, Contraindications, Effectiveness)

Brief counselling is now understood to be anything from around six to 25 sessions. Dryden and Feltham (1992, p. 4) cite a number of surveys of

Student Counselling Services in the UK where the average attendance was between two and five sessions, and another survey of mental health out-patient settings in the USA where nearly 70% of clients came for six or fewer visits. These findings indicate brief counselling by default rather than by design.

Some approaches seek to use the element of time in a constructive and deliberate way to motivate clients to face up to the source and nature of their problems. An example is Mann (1973) who might offer 12 sessions in weekly 45-minute visits. Unforeseen interruptions such as illness or bad weather would not reduce the total number of sessions offered. Right at the beginning he arranges each appointment and overtly consults his calendar so that the client can see its role in setting the exact date of their last meeting. Mann suggests that there is some evidence that a client's rate of progress may be influenced by an understanding of how long the treat-ment will last.

Brief counselling focuses on well-defined problems with modest and constrained goals. It demands a high level of counsellor skill, and is not an easier option than longer-term work. Generally, short-term counselling is suitable for clients who are not severely disturbed and who, apart from the presenting problem are func-tioning adequately in other areas of their lives. Clients tend to be actively involved, working between sessions to try out new behaviours and practise what they have learned, and be well motivated to change. Although some approaches to brief counselling make claims to the contrary, it is very doubt-ful whether it is suitable for all clients, e.g. people who have not resolved early issues concerning basic trust (Peake et al., 1988, p. 15). One risk is that they will be harmed by the experience of further loss, and that this overshadows any gain in more immediate problem management.

Brief counselling has developed largely out of economic necessity, with the pressures of increasing demands for counselling and often diminishing financial resources. However, valu-able outcomes can be achieved over relatively short periods (Budman and Gurman, 1988), so financial pressures and effectiveness are in harmony to some extent.

BRITISH ASSOCIATION FOR COUNSELLING (BAC) (See also: Accreditation, Codes of ethics, Com-plaints, Counselling)

The British Association for Counsel-ling has its roots in the Standing Conference for the Advancement of Counselling in the late 1960s and was established as a voluntary associa-tion and charity in 1977. Today it is registered as a company limited by guarantee. The rapid growth in membership reflects the increasing general interest in counselling in the UK. In 1987, BAC had 3500 individual and 250 organizational members; by 1993 this had grown to 10 000 indi-vidual and over 500 organizational members. These represent diverse views and degrees of involvement in counselling: the title of the Association embodies the idea of an association *for* counselling rather than an association of counsellors. There is an inevitable but often creative tension among different groups within the organization, with an active minority concerned with advancing the interests of practitioners in a climate of increasing professionalism both within and between counselling and psychotherapy.

BAC's published aims are concerned with 'raising the standards of counselling for the benefit of the community and recipients of counselling and promoting understanding and awareness of counselling throughout society'. BAC is now widely seen as the voice of counselling in Britain, representing its membership and client needs to government and other institutions. It has a full-time headquarters office staff and an elected Management Committee which delegates specific responsibilities to the appropriate subcommittees: Standards and Ethics, Training, Publications and Audio Visual Aids, Complaints, Research, Disability Issues, Accreditation and Recognition, Counselling and the Outer World, and the newly established Professional subcommittees.

The special interests of the membership are served by Divisions which have their own constitutions and elected executive committees. The Divisions represent different areas or settings of counselling: Association for Pastoral Care and Counselling, Association for Student Counselling, Association for Counselling at Work, Counselling in Education, Counselling in Medical Settings, Personal/Sexual/Marital/Family Counselling and Race and Cultural Education in Counselling. Membership of one or more of the Divisions runs concurrently with BAC membership. Throughout the country local groups of BAC members form Branch organizations and set up their own programme of activities.

Acceptance of the BAC Codes of Ethics and Practice is a condition of membership. There are published codes for counsellors, trainers and supervisors, and for counselling skills. Full individual members may apply for Accreditation as counsellors. In addition there are schemes for the BAC Recognition of counsellor training courses and the Recognition of supervisors. All three procedures are peer assessment schemes drawn up by members, approved by the AGM and operated by volunteer members of the Asssociation. BAC individual counsellor accreditation is increasingly required for employment as a counsellor.

The BAC Information Office provides information and advice for members and others about counselling and psychotherapy resources. The quarterly journal *Counselling* is sent free to members.

British Association for Counselling
1 Regent Place
Rugby
Warwickshire CV21 2PJ
UK

Tel: 0788 578328
Fax: 0788 562189

BRITISH ASSOCIATION OF PSYCHOTHERAPY (BAP)

BAP runs training programmes in individual psychoanalytic (Freudian) and analytical (Jungian) psychotherapy for members of the helping professions, and in child psychotherapy.

BAP
37 Mapesbury Road
London NW2 4HG
UK

Tel: 081-452 9823

BRITISH PSYCHOLOGICAL SOCIETY (BPS) (See also: Accreditation, British Association of Counselling, Codes of ethics, Professional development, Supervision)

Psychology is the major discipline underlying counselling, while counselling is a skill claimed by many of the specialist groups within Psychology: occupational, clinical, educational and counselling psychologists. The British Psychological Society (BPS) introduced a Register of Chartered Psychologists in 1990, primarily to protect the public and employers from unqualified 'psychologists'. Two differences between being a BAC-Accredited Counsellor and being a Chartered Psychologist are that a requirement of Accreditation is that 'supervision' continues (the term is used differently by the two organizations), and that Accreditation is for 5 years at a time. The two schemes are also very similar in some respects, e.g. requiring continuing professional development and agree ing to abide by the respective Codes of ethics.

Counselling Psychology is a relatively new profession in the UK, though established in the USA, Canada and Australia. The BPS Division of Counselling Psychology was set up in 1994 and signified recognition within the BPS of counselling psychology as a professional area in which training and qualifications have been developed. Two distinctive features of counselling psychology are its emphasis on the role of research in counselling practice, and a focus on well-being and development rather than on illness and clinical issues. Woolfe (1990) and Lane (1990) recognize the disputes between counsellors and counselling psychologists, and between counselling psychologists and occupational and clinical psychologists, but see the different groups as more complementary than in competition.

BPS
St Andrews House
Leicester LE1 7DR
UK

Tel: 0533 549568
Fax: 0533 470787

'BURNOUT' (See also Stress, Difficult clients, Role conflict, Support groups)

'Burnout' is a vivid but unclear term, with exhaustion probably at the core of the various definitions. Other suggested 'symptoms' include negative attitudes towards work and clients, tension and irritability, cynicism and depression. The suggested causes include too many clients, or too many 'difficult' clients, role conflict, isolation from colleagues, overlong hours and lack of a sense of control. Whether it is a useful concept, i.e. more than extreme and chronic stress, remains to be seen. What is clear is that helping people cope with psychological problems makes considerable emotional demands (Horton, 1993), and that through supervision and other means, it is possible to monitor levels of stress and take appropriate action.

C

'CASE' STUDY, *See* Supervision (presenting clients for)

CATHARSIS, *See* Anger, Emotions, Journal

CHALLENGE (*See also:* Boredom, Confrontation, Counselling, Empathy, Immediacy, Information, Patterns, Questions, Self-disclosure)

Challenges are invitations to change. The idea is to help clients move where they need to go rather than push them to where you (the counsellor) think they ought to be. The result of a challenge may be a broader horizon, deeper perceptions, or a changed point of view. Challenging is more likely to be effective if you have *earned the right* by being empathic and developing a trusting relationship; if you are open to being challenged yourself by your client; and if you listen hard to the impact of your challenge (which may after all be wholly or partly wrong or at the wrong time).

Some effective challenges involve picking up what the client has (in your view) implied, but is not very aware of:

1. **Advanced empathy:** e.g. a client talks a lot about their partner and very little about themselves, to which you might say 'You've spoken with great feeling about x's behaviour. You seem to feel overwhelmed and powerless about x'. Thus the focus of attention is brought back to your client who may move deeper into their feelings (whether your advanced empathy is accurate or not).

2. **Linking ideas** (interpretation): bringing together things your client has said and so suggesting probable patterns in their behaviour, e.g. 'you say your boss ignores you and makes you feel unwanted. I think I heard you say the same thing last week about your mother'. Essentially, you are suggesting

(very tentatively) a pattern or causal connection among various behaviours, emotions or ideas.

3. **Contrasting ideas:** e.g. 'you say you like going to the cinema with Sue, but not with Mary. I wonder what the difference is for you'.

4. **Immediacy:** e.g. 'when you stare at me like that I wonder what you are thinking and sometimes feel a bit intimidated'. This is more direct and would normally need a good deal of trust between you before saying it. More positive things are easier to say, e.g. 'I'm pleased to hear you sounding happier'.

5. **Questioning:** In our view questions should be used very sparingly in counselling. The risk is of working with what *you* are thinking about rather than staying in your *client's* frame of reference. Very often a good empathic statement is better. However, an open question can sometimes help the client move further. 'What else could you do in that situation?' or 'What else was going on for you?'

6. **Moving-on statements:** These are perhaps the simplest form of challenge, but can be very effective in helping clients move deeper into a topic. It may only be necessary to repeat one important feeling or word for your client to explore it further, e.g. 'upset'.

7. **Information giving:** *see* separate entry.

8. **Counsellor self-disclosure:** Letting a client see what others do may help them to gain a new perspective, e.g. 'what I've found helpful (but you may not) is . . .'

9. **Confrontation:** a more insistent way of challenging, *see* separate entry.

CHALLENGING, SOME GUIDELINES FOR

These guidelines are in two sections: aspects to consider challenging, and suggestions on how to challenge.

ASPECTS TO CONSIDER CHALLENGING

- What is implied; thoughts and feelings on the 'edge of clients' awareness'; what seems vague or confused; underlying meanings.
- Verbal and non-verbal mixed messages; discrepancies; contradictions, distortions, evasions or 'game playing'; blind spots.
- Resistance to change or to applying learning; failure to own problems; self-defeating behaviour; under-used strengths or resources; dysfunctional interpretations or irrational thinking.
- Transferential patterns; dynamics of relationship between counsellor and client.
- Themes, patterns, connecting 'islands'.

CHALLENGING

- Start by encouraging your client to self-challenge.
- Be tentative in the way you challenge.
- Be concrete; challenge specific examples of thoughts, feelings or

behaviours rather than making vague inferences.

- Use 'successive approximations' rather than 'all-at-once' challenges that make heavy demands on clients in a short time.
- Give time and space to respond; avoid 'hit and run' or a string of challenges, especially towards the end of sessions.
- Challenge on the basis of client values rather than your own.
- Challenge strengths and resources rather than weaknesses or deficits.
- Elicit and explore your clients reactions to any challenge; help your clients share and work through any defensive emotions.

CHANGE, *See* Effectiveness

CLASSIFICATION SYSTEMS, *See* Psychodiagnosis

CLIENTS WHO DON'T COME BACK

It can be worrying when a client does not show up, especially if you know that the client is having a lot of serious problems, or if the last session was unsatisfactory in some way. The most obvious form of positive feedback is when your clients come back, so a client not turning up can cause you to question your effectiveness as a counsellor.

Even the most experienced counsellors have clients who don't come back, or who break off the counselling relationship unexpectedly. It is important to explore your reactions in supervision, and to consider different ways in which you might contact these clients. Telephone calls can be intrusive or unwelcome. Perhaps the best way to respond is to send a brief, friendly note, enquiring after their welfare and inviting them to get in touch. If your client does not reply, we think you've been sufficiently caring and done enough; clients have the right not to reply and 'chasing after them' doesn't respect that right.

If you are particularly concerned, more direct action may be needed, but again, this is something to think through carefully in supervision. There may be times when a telephone call is necessary, or, in the last resort, a visit. But visiting clients at their home should be considered only in extreme circumstances, and should only be done after you have explored the implications in supervision.

CODES OF ETHICS (*See also:* British Association for Counselling, Counselling (BAC's Basic Principles of), Ethical dilemmas)

The main purposes of codes of ethics are to help maintain standards of counselling, to inform and protect clients, to provide a framework for counsellors to consult when trying to clarify an ethical dilemma and within which to operate a complaints procedure, to demonstrate the maturity of an organization and profession and to encourage recognition and discussion of ethical issues (Bond, 1993a, p. 12).

The following codes are available free from the British Association for Counselling (BAC):

- The Code of Ethics and Practice for Counsellors
- The Code of Ethics and Practice for the Supervision of Counsellors
- The Code of Ethics and Practice for Trainers
- The Code of Ethics and Practice for the Use of Counselling Skills

The codes have become longer and more complicated – one recent change is discussed in the entry on sexual attraction – and BAC have therefore developed a set of basic principles for counselling, which are more concise and comprehensible, especially to clients and non-practitioners.

COLLUSION (*See also:* Avoidance, Boundaries, Confrontation, Drama Triangle)

People come to counselling with many needs, some overt and others covert. Sometimes the overt needs are in opposition to the covert ones. For example a client might state that her friends are very important to her, so the overt need is to have friends, but underneath may be a fear of being left alone. In this case the covert need (which the client may or may not be aware of) is motivated by fear and the overt need is a desperate attempt to avoid the more painful covert one. It would be collusion if the counsellor concentrated solely on the client's issue with her friends. It is particularly easy to collude with avoidance if the subject is difficult for either the client or the counsellor.

COMMON FACTORS (*See also:* Core conditions, Contraindications, Counselling, Effectiveness, Emotions, Integration and eclecticism, Working alliance)

There is fairly general agreement that the main approaches to counselling work about equally well, despite radical differences in theory and techniques. One interpretation of this finding is that they have factors in common, and that these are the crucial therapeutic ingredients; however, as yet there is no clear evidence or agreement on what they are (Stiles *et al.*, 1986; Grencavage and Norcross, 1990). The most obvious common factor in all forms of counselling is the relationship between the counsellor and the client. Other common factors (which may or may not be the crucial ingredients) include new perspectives, rituals and explanations, a willingness to become actively involved in the relationship and in counselling, readiness and motivation to change, realistic expectations, and confidence in the process and in you.

Whatever approach is taken, counselling always contains opportunities for clients to disclose and work on their problems. Indeed, it often represents the first time a person has experienced being listened to and taken seriously over an extended period of time and it may very well be that this aspect of counselling is itself helpful. What counsellors actually do with what they hear may be of only secondary importance. Counselling also contains opportunities for clients to rediscover their emotions. It gives people permission to become emotional, and this might be especially important to people who are otherwise denied such opportunities.

Norcross and Grencavage (1989) refer to the identification of common factors as the most important psychotherapy trend in the 1980s. In contrast, Stiles *et al.* (1993) argue that it is stagnating, and that further research is necessary into such issues as:

- Can the common or non-specific factors of therapeutic change be more clearly specified?
- How do they operate within different theoretical approaches?
- Are there any parallels with other types of human interaction?
- How do the common factors interact with client characteristics (Shoham, in Norcross, 1993)?
- Is the distinction between common factors and specific interventions useful or are they interrelated in some way?

COMPLAINTS, ABOUT COUNSELLORS (*See also:* British Association for Counselling, Codes of ethics, Sexual attraction)

Currently there are about 20 complaints per year to BAC (BAC, 1993a). Great care is taken with them; the Complaints Subcommittee tries to be fair to both parties, and to find a balance between being 'dauntingly formal' and too informal. The overall aim is to be professional, sensitive, consistent and fair, while also upholding BAC's ethics, standards and values. Accordingly, when the Sub-

committee asks someone to take on the task of investigation/conciliation, they try to ensure that she or he is experienced in the particular area – training/education, private practice etc. – sensitive to issues of difference, and not known to the people involved. The same criteria are used in choosing members of the Adjudication Panel, if the complaint reaches that stage (BAC, 1993a).

For advice and details of the Complaints Procedure, contact BAC. For discussion see Bond (1993a).

CONCRETENESS (*See also:* Counselling, Challenge, Empathy)

Concreteness is the skill of inviting clients to be more specific. The purpose is to get below the surface communication that may not fully or accurately represent the client's experience or meaning. It also helps to ensure that you don't project your own meaning on to the client. The client has an opportunity to explain their, often idiosyncratic, definition of common feelings or experiences e.g. anger, depression, anxiety. Cormier and Cormier (1991, p. 46) identify three linguistic errors or common ways in which clients incompletely represent their experience: **deletions**, when things are left out, **distortions**, when things are not as they seem, and **generalizations**, when a total life experience or whole group of things are associated with only one feeling or event, or when conclusions are reached with no evidence.

For example, your client says 'Things are going badly'. You might respond in many ways, e.g. with a paraphrase or silence. If you chose concreteness you would say something like 'Can you give me an example?' or 'Which things'? The potential benefit is much greater clarity and therefore opportunity to empathize; the risk is sounding intrusive or like an interrogator. Concreteness therefore more often has the 'flavour' of a challenge and should be used accordingly.

CONFIDENTIALITY (*See also*: Contract, Ethical analysis, 'Good counsellors', Information, Records, Sued (being), Suicide, Supervision, Trust)

Most people (the USA figure is 69%) believe that counsellors offer absolute confidentiality (Corey and Corey, 1993, p. 319). However, counsellors and counselling organizations do not usually consider it to be an absolute. Given that you respect a client's privacy as far as you can, but that there are limits, a key question is: 'In what circumstances might you break confidentiality?' Perhaps the most problematic circumstance here is breaking confidence to protect your client's welfare or to protect another person, e.g. one who is threatened by a potentially dangerous client. Are *all* threats to be reported? And what if you have a hunch that a client is suicidal or dangerous, but no evidence? Such judgments are complicated but not uniquely so; the law rests on notions like 'reasonable care' and trusts professionals to make such judgments. On the other hand, counsellor education and training could include more

on ethical analysis (Bond, 1993a) and on coping with uncertainty.

The implications for practice are:

1. Inform clients early (as part of your contract with them) about limitations on confidentiality, e.g. what they say may be discussed with your supervisor or supervision group (though not by name and both often focus more on the counsellor than the client and are confidential themselves).
2. Tell clients about any legal or organizational factors. Some agencies require their counsellors to inform them of incest and child abuse.
3. Consult colleagues when you're unsure.
4. Records should be very brief and kept securely.
5. If you decide to break confidentiality, whenever possible discuss it with your client first, perhaps encouraging the client to inform the appropriate authority.

CONFRONTATION (*See also*: Challenge, Counselling)

Confrontation is a form of challenge in which a counsellor describes apparent distortions or discrepancies in the client's emotions, thoughts or actions. Like the other forms of challenge, it needs to be done in a responsible and caring way with clients' well-being firmly in mind. It is an attempt to help clients see something differently, and it is not directing, praising or criticizing. The following situations show when confrontation can be used:

1. **Blocking and avoiding**, e.g. 'you talk about your family quite often, but I notice you never mention your daughter'.
2. **Self-defeating attitudes and beliefs**, e.g. 'I hear you frequently calling yourself silly, which sounds as though you are being hard on yourself'. You could stop talking at this point or add: 'What evidence do you have for thinking you are silly?'
3. **Discrepancies**, e.g. 'You say you are quite happy, yet I see you here looking sad and sitting hunched up which gives a different picture.'
4. **Distortions**, e.g. 'You say everyone dislikes you'.

CONGRUENCE (*See also*: Common factors, Core conditions, Counselling, Immediacy, Self-awareness, Self-disclosure)

In Rogers' view (e.g. 1980) the congruence, or realness, of the counsellor is a determining factor in effective counselling. He warned against counsellors adopting a professional facade, or denying persistent feelings in themselves that interfere with their capacity to listen empathically. He did not mean, however, that counsellors should blurt out whatever feelings they are experiencing in an effort to be congruent. He wrote about persistent feelings, and the need to make careful decisions about how much to share in the moment, and how much should be considered later and elsewhere. These days most counsellors, particularly 'humanistic' ones, see some form of sharing their own feelings

as a natural part of the counselling relationship, providing this is done with care and sensitivity (Mearns and Thorne, 1988; Merry and Lusty, 1993).

CONTRACT, NEGOTIATING A (*See also*: Boundaries, Brief counselling, Duration, Expectations, Goals, Fees, Frequency, Information, Time boundaries, Trust)

A contract is an agreement negotiated between you and your client at the beginning of your work together. It commonly has two elements, one concerned with the purpose of counselling and your approach, the other with practical arrangements and conditions. Some counsellors prefer an informal approach, almost to the extent that it is not an explicit process. They feel that clients' understanding of what is going on, what can be achieved and how, needs to evolve gradually through their work together. Other counsellors are more formal, in some instances making use of written contracts. These may include such details as specific goals, strategies to be followed, and duration, and invite the clients to sign, thereby giving informed consent to the process. These represent extreme positions on the degree of formality of negotiating a contract.

Closely related to the issue of formality is the degree of specificity – how concrete and detailed the contract is. Some counsellors and clients agree on working towards greater self-awareness. Other contracts may be much more concrete and specify clear objectives, e.g. 'to eliminate or significantly reduce the frequency of panic attacks'. Such a contract may also identify some of the steps and strategies towards achieving this goal. Greater specificity can help to communicate a sense of direction and purpose, stimulate clear thinking and motivate the client to change. It can also provide a rational basis for evaluation. On the other hand, clients and counsellors don't always know where they are going until they get there. This is not to imply a lack of purpose, but it does make specific goals rather pointless.

The purpose and approach element is sometimes described as the counselling or treatment plan. This is a negotiated agreement about what you and your client want to achieve together and how you might work towards it. This element of the contract may follow from an initial assessment and typically is reviewed from time to time. Sometimes a more explicit form of agreement about what needs to be achieved and the strategies involved will only be relevant at a later or action-planning stage of counselling.

The 'conditions' element of the contract is intended to protect both counsellors and clients by specifying the arrangements for counselling and the boundaries within which it will take place. Part of this element will be information giving and may be non-negotiable or only negotiable within limits, for example, time and your fees. The conditions typically include the length of each session, frequency and pattern of attendance, duration of the contract, fees and time-keeping. The contract on time-keeping may involve an explicit commitment to punctuality on the part of both yourself and your clients with an additional commitment to cancel an appointment in advance rather than simply not turning up to a session. If a client arrives late, it needs to be made clear whether any additional time will be allocated. If these conditions are explicit from the very beginning they may save misunderstanding and resentment.

CONTRAINDICATIONS FOR BRIEF COUNSELLING (*See also*: Avoidance, Brief counselling, Common factors, First impressions, Referral, Trust, Working alliance)

Some clients may not be suitable for counselling and counselling isn't the answer to all psychological problems. The difficulty is judging accurately whether or not someone is likely to benefit from counselling. However, it is possible to identify various characteristics in a potential client that may serve as contraindications for brief counselling. In making such clinical judgments, it is appropriate to be cautious:

- It is not always possible to identify contraindications in the first session.
- Patterns of behaviour provide a more reliable basis than single items of evidence.
- It is important to look for evidence of the client's ability to modify or change.
- Contraindications are only indicators. There are no sharp boundaries or operational criteria that can be

used to distinguish clearly between clients who are suitable and those who are unsuitable for brief counselling.

- Many of the contraindications will be evident at some time or other in many clients and it is their degree and persistence which is important in interpreting them as valid contraindicators.
- Identifying certain characteristics may help you adjust your expectations of what might be achieved with the person in a limited period, rather than necessarily assessing him or her as unsuitable for counselling.
- Some contraindications may actually provide an initial or continuing focus for the counselling itself.

The following characteristics raise questions about a person's suitability for brief counselling, subject to the caveats discussed above.

1. **Unrealistic expectations which persist**. Some people expect counselling to give them immediate solutions to their problems, to be told what to do, to be given advice and direction. It is when such unrealistic expectations persist that they become a contraindication.

2. **No real desire to change**. Clients need, at some level, actually to want to change if counselling is to be effective. Most clients are in some way resistant to change; despite the pain and distress, they find it hard to give up troublesome aspects of their behaviour, perhaps because of hidden 'payoffs' or because they give expression to unheard parts of themselves. Some clients, especially but not necessarily involuntary clients, may show little if any willingness to change. You may find it useful to explore how and why such clients came to counselling.

3. **No clear problem**. It is hard to discover what some people want from counselling.

4. **Long history of seeking psychological help**. Some clients have seen numerous helpers over many years, and tend to have had only a few sessions with each. Typically they may also currently be seeing someone else for counselling or therapy. It may be evident that they habitually talk about their problems to everybody and anybody, but are reluctant to enter into any form of developing relationship. You may find it useful to start by exploring their views on why the other forms of helping were unsuccessful.

5. **Unresponsive clients**. Counselling is based on talking and can't make much progress, certainly in the short term, with clients who have great difficulty in talking about their experiences, and putting their thoughts and feelings into words. Here, as Jacobs (1988) points out, it is important to distinguish between those clients who lack social skills, and those who have become withdrawn and silent through depression or some trauma, and who were until recently more able to communicate actively.

6. **Avoiding emotions**. Some clients talk a lot about what they have done or are going to do, about their experiences and behaviour and more especially, other people's experiences and behaviour. It is as if the preoccupation with the story is a way of avoiding their emotions and feelings. One of the factors common to all forms of psychological therapy identified by Frank (1981), is the emotional arousal of the client, particularly during assessment. He argued that this is essential if a client is to achieve learning and associated change. If clients sustain a cool and rational view of themselves and their problems and the counselling is devoid of emotion, it is very unlikely to result in change. On the other hand, some issues are more amenable to problem-solving techniques than others and may be satisfactorily resolved by thinking them through.

7. **Inability to relate to others**. Most approaches to counselling place a high value on the need to establish an effective working relationship. You can look for evidence of a capacity to relate to others, irrespective of whether the relationship was experienced as positive or negative. It is unlikely that clients who have found it very difficult to relate either well or badly to others will find it possible to form a working relationship with you.

8. **Lack of capacity to trust**. People vary in the time it takes for them to learn to trust others. The capacity to trust is essential in order for the client to be open and revealing of very personal problems and concerns. Clients will test whether they can trust you in a variety of ways – often by asking questions – but may not be consciously aware of what they are doing or why they are doing it. While counsellors should not want to foster a dependent relationship, clients need to place some reliance on the counsellor and counselling. Fiercely independent clients won't stay long. Indications of this are the request for only occasional counselling sessions, or clients who persistently 'yes but'. Other clients find any face-to-face relationship too intimate and threatening. They too tend to drop out of brief counselling.

9. **People who are too dependent**. People who depend on a high dosage of drugs to carry on with their day-to-day routine are unlikely to benefit from brief counselling. Another form of dependence is on the counsellor and counselling. Clients need to be able to tolerate painful feelings and feel secure enough to be able to cope with life between sessions.

10. **Reluctance to accept responsibility**. While many people come to counselling wanting other people or their circumstances to change, counselling can only work towards helping them change the way they themselves feel, think

or behave. Some people seem unable to see the ways in which they might be contributing to their own difficulties or the ways in which they might change, and typically lack empathy with others.

11. **Out of touch with reality.** Disturbing and irrational thoughts and behaviour which make it difficult for a person to manage everyday life are a further contra-indication. The key criterion is the extent to which they are actually aware of what is going on. Some people with these characteristics are quite unaware of the implications of their behaviour and the havoc caused in their lives as well as in the lives of those around them. Others seem unable to tolerate their disturbing thoughts and feelings and seriously fear that they are 'going mad'. A sometimes related pattern of behaviour is the way some people flit from one subject to another (Jacobs, 1988).

CORE CONDITIONS (*See also*: Congruence, Counselling, Empathy, Power, Respect)

The term 'core conditions' is generally associated with client-centred (or person-centred) counselling. Rogers (e.g. 1957, 1980) believed that effective counselling was most likely when the counsellor was able to offer clients a relationship rich in the qualities of empathy, congruence and unconditional positive regard. However, although most forms of counselling would agree that these three counsellor qualities are necessary, only client-centred counselling regards them as both necessary and sufficient. In other words, Rogers argued that the relationship that develops between counsellor and client is the most significant agent of change, not the counsellor's repertoire of techniques. This remains a controversial point of view (e.g. Patterson, 1984). Research has tended to support the necessity rather than the sufficiency of the core conditions. Hill and Corbett (1993) concluded that the debate about the core conditions is unresolved: 'Researchers will need to clarify what they mean by constructs such as empathy and develop more sophisticated measures and methods' (p. 8).

Rogers justified his position on three grounds. First, he argued that people have within them the personal resources they need for positive personality change, and that no-one is in a position to supply these resources from the outside. Second, emotional or psychological problems stem from childhood experiences in which 'conditions of worth' are internalized as a result of the negative judgements of others. Client-centred counsellors aim to provide a relationship in which negative conditioning in this sense can be brought into the client's awareness, and provided the client is empathically understood by someone trustworthy and non-judgemental, these conditions of worth can be replaced with more contemporary and personal evaluations. Third, Rogers was committed to the position that the counselling relationship should be as egalitarian as possible with power being shared (ideally, equally) by client and counsellor. Rogers believed this position would be undermined if clients were to become dependent on the counsellor's techniques, rather than discovering their own internal resources (Mearns and Thorne, 1988; Merry and Lusty, 1993).

CORE MODEL (*See also*: Counselling, Theory)

One of the guiding concepts of counsellor education and training is that it should provide substantial grounding in a 'core theoretical model' (BAC, 1990b). This model should be reflected in the theory, skills and client work of a course and in the way it is structured, assessed, taught and administered. A core model that underpins a training programme provides coherence and internal consistency both within the training and in the counsellors' subsequent practice. On developing and continuing to develop your personal model of counselling, see Elton Wilson (1993), Inskipp (1993), Ivey *et al.* (1993).

COST-EFFECTIVENESS, OF COUNSELLING, *See* Effectiveness

COUNSELLING (*See also*: Beginnings, Core model, Core qualities, Frameworks, Integration and eclecticism, Psychological type, Readiness to change, Referral, Theories)

One approach to defining 'counselling' is to distinguish between different kinds of counselling, e.g. between (i) counselling for personal growth, with people who are functioning well in most respects, and (ii) counselling with severely distressed people. Other systems for describing counselling are based on theories or kinds of problem (e.g. Woolfe *et al.*, 1989; Dryden, 1990; Corey, 1991; Ivey *et al.*, 1993). The systems can help to clarify what counselling is and is not, both for yourself and for others – and therefore when to offer counselling to someone, and when to suggest referral.

The model of counselling outlined below is consistent with the work of Brammer *et al.* (1993), Egan (1975), Ivey *et al.* (1987, 1993), Lang *et al.* (1990) and others. It is also defined more simply in several entries, including those on Common factors, Frameworks and Journal (writing a).

AN INTEGRATIVE PROCESS MODEL OF COUNSELLING

By 'integrative process model', we mean that it provides a model of the process through which counsellor and client work together, but without implying any one theory of personality or human development. Rather, it provides an organizing framework for integrating concepts and techniques from other approaches. Alternatively, it can 'stand alone' as an approach to counselling. It requires an understanding of the counselling process, a range of communication skills and an awareness of when to use specific strategies and skills (Ivey *et al.*, 1987, 1993; Egan, 1990; Mahalik, 1990).

Table 2: Summary of an integrative process model of counselling

Theme	Stage 1 tasks	Stage 2 tasks	Stage 3 tasks
1. Relationship	Establish a working alliance	Maintain and use the relationship	Deal with issues around ending the relationship
2. Content	Explore, and make an initial assessment	Work towards learning and changing	Consolidate and apply learning
3. Planning and reflection	Develop a therapeutic plan	Monitor and revise plan. Reflect on process	Evaluate process and outcomes

Three developmental and inter-related themes – the Relationship, Content and Planning – run through each of the three broadly defined stages of the model. Each stage is characterized by the need to achieve particular 'tasks'. The model can be summarized in a matrix of themes and stages (Table 2).

The developing relationship between the counsellor and client is the first theme. In Stage One, the task is to establish an effective working alliance. The counsellor is empathic, accepting and congruent and this is seen as therapeutic and sometimes sufficient. In Stage Two the quality of the relationship is maintained and the main task is to facilitate change. Stage Three is concerned with ending the relationship.

The second theme is the content of the client's problem or problems. In Stage One the counsellor helps the client explore and define one problem. In Stage Two the main task is to facilitate learning and change, with counsellor and client working towards a deeper understanding, exploring different ways of thinking, feeling and/or behaving, and perhaps identifying goals and ways of achieving them. In Stage Three, the task is to work with the client to consolidate and generalize new ways of being or behaving.

The third theme running through each stage is planning and reflection. This is concerned with articulating goals and strategies and with reflection and evaluation, both with the client and internally, as a 'reflective practitioner' (Horton, 1993). Two kinds of goals are identified: those concerned with helping the client to discover solutions or, more typically, specific action plans for coping with or managing immediate problems, and second, broader goals such as developing a stronger sense of personal identity.

The model makes a distinction between strategies and skills. Strategies are ways of achieving particular tasks, while skills are the behaviours (interventions or responses) for actually doing so. For example, the task of establishing a working alliance is achieved by communicating the 'core qualities' while the strategy is implemented by using the skills of active listening. The strategies and skills are essential tools, which provide a set of logical and practical guidelines, but they are not an end in themselves. Rather, they need to be integrated into counselling through the quality of the relationship.

The model makes explicit the tasks for each stage of counselling. Its function is to provide a sense of direction and purpose, a kind of 'cognitive map with delivery potential' (Egan, 1975) which is intended to help the counsellor and client plan, monitor and evaluate. It is not intended as a ready to apply mechanistic formula. Similarly, while the stages are developmental and sequential, the model does not imply a linear progression. As new needs or different aspects of the problem emerge, the actual process, especially around the content theme, will continually move backwards and forwards within the organizing framework.

The model's rationale is based on assumptions in two areas – human development and the counselling process. Three key assumptions are summarized next:

1. Psychological problems are regarded as multidimensional and seldom attributable to one source, situation or factor. It is assumed that people are too complex to be explained by any one theory, and that social context plays an important part (Brammer et al., 1993).

2. It is possible to identify common steps and stages in the counselling process, irrespective of the counsellor's theoretical orientation (Ivey et al., 1987, 1993; Beitman, 1990; Lang et al., 1990; Brammer et al., 1993). On this basis the concept of a model of process can be used as an integrating framework. This is a form of systematic eclecticism or what Brammer refers to as a creative synthesis approach to theory. The principles and criteria for integration are expanded in Lebow (1987) and Brammer et al. (1993).

3. It is essential for counsellors to develop the necessary personal qualities and skills to counsel effectively. To have a map of the process is not enough; counsellors need to be able to select appropriate strategies and explanatory concepts for assessment and change, and have the skills to implement them.

COUNSELLING, BAC BASIC PRINCIPLES OF (*See also*: Codes of ethics, Complaints, Counselling)

BAC developed the set of principles shown in Table 3 mainly with clients in mind, but also as a statement representing BAC members' very diverse approaches to counselling. The principles are spelled out in more detail, but less accessibly, in the Codes of ethics.

Table 3 Basic principles of counselling (from BAC, 1993b)

1. The aim of counselling is to provide an opportunity for a client to work towards living in a more satisfying and resourceful way.
2. Counselling is voluntarily and deliberately undertaken by counsellor and client. It is different from other ways of helping.
3. Before counselling starts, the counsellor clarifies with the client the basis on which counselling is to be given, including method, duration, fees and confidentiality; changes can subsequently be made only with the agreement of the client.
4. In counselling the right of the client to make his or her own decisions is respected.
5. Counsellors continually monitor their own skills, experience, resources and practice.
6. Counsellors will be properly trained for their roles and be committed to maintaining their competence.
7. Counsellors will not misrepresent their training or experience.
8. Counsellors have regular and appropriate supervision/consultative support.
9. Counsellors do not abuse their position of trust financially, emotionally or sexually.
10. All that takes place between counsellor and client is treated with respect and discretion.

COUNTER-TRANSFERENCE (*See also*: Emotions, First impressions, Process, Self-awareness, Supervision, Transference)

Counter-transference is a psychoanalytic term, referring to the counsellor's unconscious reaction to a client, confusing her or him with someone else, and thus distorting their judgment and ability to empathize (Jacobs, 1988; Hawkins and Shohet, 1989). Stewart (1992) suggests several indicators, e.g. preoccupation with a particular client, in the form of daydreams or fantasies; behaving differently towards them (more lenient, more strict); and not wanting to end (pp. 56–57). Whatever your theoretical orientation, and whether or not you use the term counter-transference, it is important to explore your reactions to clients in supervision.

CROSS-CULTURAL, *See* Multi-culturalism

CRISIS, FOR THE COUNSELLOR (*See also*: 'Burnout', Congruence, Core conditions, Referral, Self-disclosure, Stress, Support groups, Supervision)

Counsellors often feel that, no matter what they are going through in their personal lives, they should always be available and helpful to clients. There is an expectation that counsellors can leave their personal concerns behind when they enter the counselling room, and to a great extent, this expectation is a reasonable one. But when counsellors do experience problems in their own lives and if these are very difficult or even overwhelming, they are very likely to affect the counsellor's ability to give full attention to the concerns of others. At such times, counsellors can feel uncertain about whether they should say anything about their personal troubles (perhaps in the name of 'congruence'), or at what point it is advisable to cease offering counselling altogether until personal problems have been resolved.

Some approaches, particularly those with a psychodynamic orientation, suggest there should be very little self-disclosure or none at all. Client-centred counsellors tend to be more self-disclosing, but even so would not wish their self-disclosure to shift the focus of counselling away from their clients to the counsellor. The most unhelpful thing of all would be to draw clients into your own personal life and its problems so that clients became distracted from their own concerns. This would also be unethical.

In times of crisis, the strength of your support network becomes crucial. If immediate colleagues are not approachable or are unavailable, your supervisor would usually be the first person to whom you turn for professional advice and support. Your supervisor should be able to help you separate those issues which are of a personal nature and best dealt with through your own counselling (or by other means), and those which are professional and ethical issues. The decision about whether to take a break from counselling needs to be explored in supervision also. BAC accepts a period of up to 6 months away from counselling without affecting your chances of re-accreditation.

Lambers (1993) recognizes that counsellors are inevitably reminded by clients of their own unresolved problems, though often as a 'vague awareness' at first. She gives six questions for possible use in supervision. Essentially these focus on the core conditions. She also suggests other relevant questions about the impact on the client and about what the counsellor might do.

CRISIS COUNSELLING (*See also*: Crying, Depression, Emotions, Empathy, Guidance, Literal description, Psychological type, Referral)

The word crisis is usually applied to immediately threatening and highly stressful situations which seem to demand some urgent response or action. People typically feel overwhelmed by stress and unable to cope and often angry, fearful and despairing. In crisis, people face a situation that upsets their characteristic patterns of thought and behaviour. Their habitual ways of responding to and dealing with problems are insufficient, though Moos (1991) suggests that as people cannot remain in a state of disequilibrium a crisis is necessarily self-limiting. By definition a crisis is a turning point, and some (even temporary) resolution will be found. The resolution may be a healthy adaptation or foreshadow further problems.

Crisis counselling differs from other forms of counselling in several ways (Morley *et al.*, 1967).

1. It tends not to be based on any particular theoretical orientation or school.

2. The goal is resolution of the immediate crisis and restoring the individual's normal level of functioning.

3. There is relatively little concern with the client's past and then only when it may help to understand their response to the present crisis. Problems of symptoms not directly related to the crisis are not dealt with.

4. It tends to be brief and intense, with the client being seen more than once a week. The counsellor may take a more active and sometimes more directive role than usual.

5. It can involve general support, direct encouragement of adaptive behaviour and practical steps taken on behalf of the client. Techniques and strategies vary, limited only by the counsellor's flexibility and creativity.

6. Crisis counselling often involves the client's family members, close friends or other social support network.

Four major goals and three 'balancing factors' seem prominent in the literature (e.g. Worden, 1984; Moos, 1991). In crisis counselling, the counsellor aims to accomplish the goals through helping the client with the three factors. Their relative presence or absence seems to determine an individual's ability to deal with crisis and whether their return to equilibrium is likely to result in a healthy or problematic adaptation.

The goals are:

1. to understand the personal meaning and significance of the situation;

2. to preserve or encourage a positive self-image by confronting and accepting the reality of the situation;

3. to experience the painful emotions and re-establish a reasonable emotional balance;

4. to maintain a sense of competence by adjusting to the environment and responding to the crisis.

The related 'balancing factors' are as follows:

1. **Realistic perception of the situation.** If someone has a realistic perception of what has happened, and can recognize the relationship between the crisis and their feelings of stress, then attempts to manage the problem and reduce the level of stress are more likely to be effective.

2. **Adequate coping resources.** Throughout their life people learn to cope with difficult situations in many different and individual ways. These skills and strategies can focus on finding meaning, coping with the practical aspects of dealing with the emotions linked to the crisis.

3. **Basic human support.** People are social beings and there is good evidence to suggest that the existence of a natural support network of family and friends, and the person's ability actually to make use of it, have a vital role in outcome (Raphael, 1984; Duck, 1992).

Crisis counselling may also involve helping the client understand the nature of the crisis. Parry (1990), Moos (1991) and others have identified several variables that help define a crisis and the nature of its impact on the individual:

- **Focus**. Was the person directly involved or did it happen to someone else?
- **Predictability**. Was it unexpected or was it possible to predict that it was going to happen?
- **Intensity**. How suddenly did it all happen? Was there any warning? How long did it last?
- **Choice**. Did the person voluntarily enter the situation that resulted in a crisis. For example choosing to separate from a partner may end up as a traumatic situation.
- **Pervasiveness**. Does the crisis permeate many different areas of the person's life or is it contained within one area?
- **Magnitude**. How unfamiliar or different was the new situation? To what extent did it disrupt the routine pattern of living?
- **Controllability**. Once the crisis happened, did the person feel they could do anything at all that might help in some way?
- **Risk**. Was there any threat or danger?
- **Distress**. Was there any pain, suffering or humiliation?
- **Revelation**. Was anything negative revealed during or as a result of the crisis?
- **Loss**. Loss is part of all crisis situations – the loss of things as they were before the crisis. 'Loss' here is a very general term, e.g. of status, independence, role or relationship, identity, valued possession or ideal, a loved person and so on. Reactions to loss vary considerably (Wortman and Silver, 1989).

In addition to these 11 factors, Moos (1991) identifies demographic, personal, physical and social environmental variables that may also affect the outcome and influence the person's appraisal of the crisis, the nature of the specific tasks and the choice of strategies.

GUIDELINES

The basic steps in crisis counselling are assessment, planning and intervention.

1. **Assessment**. The first clinical judgement is whether the person should receive immediate and intensive support. This decision is based on an assessment of first, the likelihood of any imminent danger to the person or other people and second, whether the individual is able to maintain normal responsibilities and obligations or whether these should be temporarily and explicitly transferred to others.

   The assessment then moves on to examine, often in great detail, the precipitating event(s) and the effects of the resulting crisis. The purpose is to understand what has happened and assess the person's ability to cope with the situation. It is often some time before the precise nature and full extent of the crisis is recognized. It can be useful to encourage the client to talk through what has happened over the previous 48 hours or so. Assessment is basically concerned with gathering information.

2. **Planning**. This step is about identifying the central issues. Priorities and goals are decided. Alternative strategies and solutions to reduce the effects of crisis are generated and the best options chosen. Tentative explanations are put forward to account for the individual's reaction.

3. **Intervention**. After the necessary data are collected, the focus is on the immediate situation and possible ways forward. The client needs to leave the first session with some positive guidelines for coping. These are evaluated and revised in subsequent sessions. Later sessions work on anticipatory planning and developing realistic goals for the future. The counsellor and client continue to work towards resolution of the crisis and may, at least initially, meet several times a week.

CHECKLIST

This is a checklist of principles and strategies for crisis counselling (adapted from Worden, 1984, pp. 39–48). Their effectiveness depends on a high level of trust and the quality of the relationship between the counsellor and client.

1. **Facilitating the expression of emotion**. Family, culture or personality type may inhibit the expression of emotion, which can block the effective resolution of a crisis and be very destructive.

2. **Assurance of normality**. Some people need to be reassured that they are not losing their sanity. An acute sense of distraction, total preoccupation with what happened and hallucinations are examples of common and normal responses to a crisis. It is also important to allow for a very wide range of individual reactions.

3. **Recognizing chronic reactions**. This is the other side of the need to reassure the person that their behaviour is quite normal. Counsellors need to remain alert to chronic or pathological reactions and the possible need for referral.

4. **Encouraging a realistic perception**. This is about helping the client establish the personal meaning and significance of what has happened. It is understanding and accepting the reality of the crisis and what it means for the future, and may involve going over the memories and circumstances many times. Literal description can be useful, and in itself can reduce distress and have therapeutic value. A realistic perception is necessary for problem-management.

5. **Facilitating emotional withdrawal**. It is essential to help the client let go of the past and recognize that things are different and will never be the same again. Exploring previously relevant experiences can be helpful. It is not the same as forgetting – clients may want to hold on to memories, and painful and distressing episodes will re-occur – but it is about investing some emotional energy in the future and in new ways of living.

6. **Evaluating coping strategies.** Some coping strategies and defences are useful, at least for a limited period. However, others e.g. excessive use of alcohol or other drugs, bring problems of their own. Clients can be encouraged to explore their coping behaviour, evaluate its effectiveness and consider alternatives.

7. **Adjusting to the new situation.** People who have been through a crisis may need help to adjust to the changed situation. They may need to work through their emotions in familiar surroundings and should be discouraged from immediately making major life decisions, e.g. selling their home and moving.

    It may be helpful to encourage people to pay attention to looking after themselves, eating, taking exercise, discovering 'anchor points' in their day and developing a routine. Anticipating possible low points in the day or critical points in the future (e.g. anniversaries and special days) and exploring possible ways of minimizing their impact can also be useful.

8. **Allowing time to re-adjust.** There is a tendency for people to feel that they should get over the crisis quickly; there is often social pressure from others to recover from the loss and pain of the crisis and return to a normal routine. However, the process can be a gradual one, and for some it will take many months or years. Conversely, for other people, distress is neither inevitable nor necessary (Wortman and Silver, 1989).

9. **Continuing social support.** Exploring possible ways of developing and maintaining an adequate social support network is an important part of crisis work.

10. **Facilitating problem-solving.** This is the essence of crisis counselling. It is about helping the person to make decisions and manage problems. Egan (1990) identifies some clear steps in the process:
    (a) Identify and define the problem.
    (b) Establish priorities.
    (c) Specify desired goals or outcomes.
    (d) Generate possible action plans or strategies.
    (e) Mentally rehearse each alternative and the possible consequences.
    (f) Select one alternative.
    (g) Implement, step by step.
    (h) Evaluate and revise as appropriate.

CRYING (*See also*: Depression, Emotions, Touch)

When clients cry, it is tempting but of course unhelpful to distract them with a cup of tea or other form of comfort or sympathy, even though this is a natural response to people in distress. Counselling helps people explore the depth of their present emotions, however distressing and painful they are. More subtly, it is also unhelpful to believe that people *should* cry, and that if they don't there must be something wrong either with them, or with you as a counsellor. Mills and Wooster (1987) make the useful point here that individuals vary greatly in the form their crying takes at its *peak*: from watery eyes to silent weeping to noisy sobbing and wailing.

Some people feel very uncomfortable or embarrassed with clients who cry, or who begin to express very deep or powerful emotions, and you may have different expectations of women and men in these respects. It can be difficult to stay with someone in very deep distress without wanting to interfere, and you can begin to feel very distressed yourself sometimes. If this does seem to happen, you may be over-identifying with your client, or some deep emotions in yourself may be being re-stimulated. Discussion with your supervisor, counselling for yourself, or both, are probably the best actions to take.

D

DENIAL (*See also*: Abuse, Avoidance, Challenge, Collusion, Empathy, Interpersonal Process Recall)

Some parts of each of us are difficult to look at or 'own' and we may therefore deny their existence or their full significance. Usually there is a fearful or upsetting experience behind the denial; particularly painful times may have been suppressed beyond easy recall. If you think a client is denying something, it is better not to be persistent in trying to unearth the problem, as the client may become more defensive and put up further barriers.

Prevention is probably the best approach to conscious denial, through helping clients feel safer and less threatened, listening to the underlying sense of what is said, and reflecting back any unease. Part of the contract between you can include an agreement that the client can say if there is something they don't want to talk about and that the counsellor will respect that wish. By feeling safe, clients are then able to face up to and talk about the subject they at first wanted to avoid, without being pushed into a situation of denial. Some clients are helped by exploring their difficulty in talking about a topic rather than the topic itself.

Unconscious denial is perhaps more difficult, as its existence to begin with is unknown both to client and counsellor. It often involves incidents from childhood which are too painful to remember. Good empathic skills, so that the client learns how to trust and feel safe, gradually allow the memories and emotions to surface.

Sometimes a client denies a gentle challenge, e.g. 'it sounds as though you find endings difficult'. 'No I don't'. They may be right or they may be denying the loss and pain in ending. In either case it is usually best to accept what the client says. The challenge might however have triggered something in the client and, as they reflect, they realize that actually endings *are* difficult for them. The topic of difficult endings might also surface again during another session and then the counsellor could link the two incidents, so perhaps enabling the client to explore further.

DEPRESSION (*See also*: Books (self-help), Crying, Suicide, Thoughts)

Depression may mean anything from temporarily feeling 'down' to being so debilitated as to be unable to move or speak. Anxious or angry clients may also be quite depressed. Counselling usually involves trying to enable clients to express the underlying feelings which have been suppressed, or to learn to think in a more positive manner. One of the traps for the counsellor is to take on to themselves the feelings of despair in the client (whether overtly expressed or not) to such an extent that they too feel hopeless.

Cognitive counselling appears to be particularly helpful with depression (e.g. Clayton and Barrett, 1983; Barker, 1992; Gilbert, 1992). It involves helping clients change their negative automatic thoughts into more positive ones and also recording what gives them pleasure and what they achieve. It is assumed that once the initial negative cycle is broken it is then easier to help the client explore the underlying problems and suppressed feelings which caused the difficulty in the first place.

Barker's (1992) book includes a self-help guide on depression using Beck's and Ellis's ideas, and with the following unusual features: it is written in the first person, to try to encourage receptivity and a sense of personal responsibility; the reading level is equivalent to a tabloid newspaper; and the publishers have waived copyright on it. The guide is also published separately (Barker, 1993).

Radically different views and methods of working with depression are put forward by Storr (1990) and by Bugental and Bugental (1980). Storr sees a need to help depressed people 'disinter' the active, aggressive elements of themselves, for example by discussing their feelings towards their parents, who they're likely to see as perfect. Bugental argues that a period of depression can be healing, and a valuable signal that change is needed. He helps clients to 'go with' depression and rest, patiently and acceptingly, simplifying life and treating depression as important to well-being. Sutherland (1987) provides a sharp, vivid, considered account of his own depression and experience of a variety of treatments.

DIAGNOSIS, *See* Assessment, Psychodiagnosis

DIFFERENCES BETWEEN CLIENTS AND COUNSELLORS, *See* Multiculturalism

DIFFICULT CLIENTS (*See also*: Contraindications for Brief Counselling, Drama Triangle, Empathy, Referral)

Difficult clients are those whom you

find particularly challenging. Specific difficulties are covered elsewhere, but general strategies for coping with difficult clients include:

- presenting your difficulties openly to your supervisor or supervision group;
- asking yourself what, exactly, you find difficult about this client;
- exploring to what extent this client reminds you of people you have found difficult in the past;
- reflecting on the quality of the relationship you are able to offer to this client;
- making a distinction between what clients say to you, and the ways in which they express themselves. For example, you may 'switch off' to a client who swears or who repeats themselves a lot, but they are still expressing themselves, perhaps the best way they can, and you can try to focus on that, rather than on the language itself;
- similarly, making a distinction between clients whose values are unacceptable to you and professional responsibility (Walker, 1993);
- looking to see if there are common features of the clients you find difficult, or recurring 'themes'. Again, these are issues that may be explored with your supervisor or in your personal counselling;
- try to distinguish between the person and the quality or behaviour you find difficult.

You may find it very difficult to counsel some clients, however hard you try. In such circumstances, it may be better to refer them. It is, of course, advisable to discuss how you do this in supervision, so that you do it as constructively as possible.

DIFFICULTIES, IN BEING A CLIENT

(See also: Avoidance, Contract, Expectations, Fees, Multiculturalism, Respect, Trust)

Many clients come to us at times when they have difficulties making any decision, including the decision to seek help. Some clients feel a sense of failure, that they ought to be able to take care of themselves, and this in itself may lower a client's already threatened sense of self-esteem. Your client may have had to overcome much resistance and prejudice before coming to see you, and this makes the first few minutes of your first session even more important. Treating any expression of fear, anxiety or resistance with empathy will help your client feel that you respect their doubts, and will also help to establish trust in your capacity to understand.

People from some cultural groups may find it especially difficult to talk in personal terms to complete strangers. You need to be patient and understanding here, particularly if you are not familiar with your client's cultural traditions and norms. Some clients also have to overcome strong feelings of guilt or disloyalty to members of their families before they can talk openly. Other factors that can create difficulties include time commitment and travelling distance. These may be a sign of avoidance, which you can offer to help the client explore; otherwise there is not much you can do, and the final decision about whether to continue or not will have to be left to your client.

The key question is: what could make counselling easier for your client? If you can arrange to see clients at times when they do not have to spend time alone in dark railway stations or bus stops, or have to walk far after dark, this may help a lot. Similarly, people who cannot negotiate stairs or who are in wheelchairs obviously find many buildings and streets difficult. What you can do to an old building or to a private house to make access easier will be limited, but the removal of obstacles from hallways, and the provision of a wooden ramp to help negotiate steps, both make a contribution.

Once a client has decided to start counselling with you, there can still be difficulties in continuing. Finance may have a part to play in this, and if you operate a sliding scale according to clients' ability to pay, your client may ask to renegotiate this part of the contract. How you respond to this will be a personal decision, but decisive factors could include: your own income level; a point below which you are not prepared to go; a point at which you feel exploited.

DILEMMAS FOR COUNSELLORS
(See also: Mistakes)

Dryden (1985) is a collection of interviews with counsellors and therapists about dilemmas they have experienced in their counselling. Each interview focuses on a particular kind of dilemma, e.g. 'giving warmth or love to clients' (with Albert Ellis), 'boundaries' (Brian Thorne), the 'non-improving patient' (Paul Wachtel).

DISABILITIES, See Multiculturalism

DRAMA TRIANGLE (See also: Collusion, Immediacy, Self-awareness)

The 'Drama Triangle' (Karpman, 1968) is a model which some counsellors and clients find useful in explaining certain patterns in behaviour, especially between two people. It suggests three complementary roles: Victim, Rescuer and Persecutor. Example of the roles as brief, normal responses are seeing pictures on the television of starving children (victims) and immediately writing out a cheque to help their cause (rescuer), and being ill (victim), which may bring someone to look after us (rescuer) and lead to a colleague being angry with us (persecutor), as they have to do our work. These examples show normal behaviour; the people concerned don't carry on and on in the same roles and therefore don't become caught in the drama triangle.

Problems occur when people are stuck, either in one of the roles, or else going round and round the triangle, drawing in others. A classic Victim role is taken by someone who feels, or actually is, hard done by and seems constantly being put upon. Some people get angry with them (Persecutor), others might try to help (Rescuer), but nothing seems to change matters. The original Victim may then alternate to Persecutor, blaming the others, who may then become Victims.

People who get caught in the triangle, in whatever role, very often have low self-esteem and see themselves as having little control over their lives. Others may view them differently and perceive them as being very powerful or frustrating as they stay firmly in their role in the triangle. Counsellors can try to help them increase their self-esteem, become more self-sufficient, and escape from the trap. However the more the client is stuck in their role in the triangle the easier it is for the counsellor to be trapped as well. Some clients make it very difficult for the counsellor to resist telling them what to do, or doing things for them (rescuing), while others leave the counsellor feeling angry (persecuting). If the counsellor is unaware of this and gets caught in the triangle, the client is again pushed into the Victim role, the place which is so familiar to them. So the triangle continues, even within the counselling relationship.

DRAWINGS, *See* Life Space Diagram, Journal, Paper and pencil exercises

DRINKS/REFRESHMENTS

The way you establish or fail to establish a concentrated and 'focused' mood may affect the counselling process significantly. Offering drinks and other refreshments to clients can cause problems in this respect. If you work in a place with a waiting room and/or receptionist, it is possible to supply refreshments in a way that is unobtrusive and does not interfere with the counselling process. However, if you work on your own, and your refreshment facilities are in your counselling room it can be quite distracting for clients if their counsellor spends time filling kettles, washing cups, etc. There is also the problem of what to say while this process is going on. Do you start 'counselling' while making drinks, or engage in 'small talk'?

A further problem is that on the one hand a drink can help clients relax, but on the other it can become something to hold and 'hide behind', with clients feeling exposed when they put the cup down. However, if you can prepare a drink with the minimum of fuss, there seems to be no real reason why you should not offer one to your client, especially on a very cold or hot day or when the client has had a long journey. Having drinking water readily available is a helpful idea, especially as increases in adrenaline can make the throat very dry.

DROPOUT, *See* Clients who don't come back

DRUNK AND/OR DRUGGED CLIENTS (*See also*: Anger, Boundaries, Emotions, Violence and its prevention)

If you work for an agency that specializes in treating people who misuse alcohol or other drugs, you will have a clear protocol (procedure) for dealing with a drunk client or one who has obviously recently taken a drug other than alcohol. A problem for the generic counsellor is to be confronted with a client who is drunk or drugged when this is not a familiar state to you. The behaviour of a drunk person or a person under the influence of other drugs can be unpredictable, threatening or frightening. If your client does become aggressive or threatening, or behaves unpredictably, get help if necessary as calmly and quietly as you can.

All drugs affect a person's behaviour and perceptions to some degree. Some prescribed drugs may, for some people, reduce their anxiety sufficiently to allow counselling to take place. On the other hand, an obviously drunk or drugged client is unlikely to be in a suitable frame of mind for counselling. If you have reason to believe a client is affected by drugs you can try to explain to them that counselling is unlikely to be effective under such circumstances, and that it is better to postpone this session rather than continue with it. If your client is not receptive to this advice, you may decide to try to continue, even though any counselling is likely to be a waste of effort. You can discuss the issue later with your client when he or she is not influenced by drugs. It is probably advisable to be clear at this point that you will not attempt to continue with counselling whenever the client is using any drugs, including alcohol.

A further consideration is that you may be open to prosecution if you knowingly allow your premises to be used for taking a controlled drug.

DURATION (*See also*: Brief counselling, Contract, Endings)

Counselling was originally conceived as a process that 'takes a long time', but in recent years, against a background of economic constraints and concerns about the allocation of resources, there has been growing pressure for short-term counselling. Moreoever, although there are conflicting views, there is no current research which suggests that the longer counselling goes on for the better or more effective it is. Indeed, some research seems rather to support the value of short-term counselling (e.g. Barkham, 1990, 1993b). Time-limited and Brief counselling approaches have therefore emerged within various theoretical positions in an attempt to make counselling less expensive and more available, and the typical length of time people actually remain in counselling is between 6–8 sessions (Garfield, 1989).

The term 'Brief counselling' is usually taken to describe anything up to 25 sessions. 'Time-limited' counselling is a variation; it specifies the actual number of sessions at the start of counselling, e.g. once a week for say 12 sessions. There are of course various patterns of counselling contract. Fifteen sessions, for example, may either be consecutive weekly sessions or spread over a year.

The duration of counselling may be influenced by several factors including your own preference, experience and training; agency policy restricting the length of time for each client; the nature of the presenting problem – with more severely disturbed clients taking longer; the desired goals and outcomes; and the extent to which it is possible to identify limited aims and focus on specific issues or 'focal concerns'.

E

ECLECTICISM, *See* Integration and eclecticism

EFFECTIVENESS OF COUNSELLING

(*See also*: Common factors, Counselling, Journal, Research)

It is now firmly established that counselling is effective (Stiles *et al.*, 1986; Barkham, 1990, 1993a), though this statement needs qualifying. For example the degree of effectiveness is generally seen by researchers – perhaps unfairly – as modest, in tune with Freud's remark about transforming 'neurotic misery' into 'common unhappiness'. The unfairness lies in expecting radical change, as if counselling was like re-programming a computer or washing out a test-tube. Zilbergeld (1983) argued that we usually hear only the dramatic success stories, that success is reducing the intensity of a problem – a depressed person becomes calm or depressed less often rather than exuberant – and that many problems are better seen as normal human variation.

A number of researchers have argued that the effectiveness of counselling only appears to be modest. It depends what you compare it with. For example, Rosenthal (1990) discussed an acclaimed study of the effects of aspirin on reducing heart attacks. The reduction in number of heart attacks was 4%, i.e. four people in a hundred, on average, would improve (avoid a heart attack) through taking aspirin. He then points out that the average effect size for counselling is about 10% and that this is by these standards considerably better than 'modest'. Rosenthal's way of presenting the data however is less clear; psychology still lacks a generally agreed way of presenting data on practical significance.

Gallo (1978) described two hypothetical situations that have the same effect size as counselling, i.e. about 10%. In the first, assume that the average life-expectancy of someone who is 40 years old now is 70, and that a treatment lasting as long as, and costing the same as, counselling raises the life expectancy by 10%. Seven extra years of life (assuming equal quality of life) would be highly cost-effective! The second situation is a device fitted to a car for the same cost as counselling and improving mileage by 10%: at 15 000 miles per year and USA prices, it would take 22 years to pay for itself. The same effect size is therefore enormously important or trivial, depending on the context.

The question of whether counselling is 'worth the effort and expense' needs three pieces of information (Gallo, 1978):

1. its cost;
2. the benefits;
3. the benefits of alternative courses of action.

A fourth factor could also be included: the risk of deterioration. Several studies in organizations seem to have shown substantial benefits, e.g. an over 50% reduction in absence from work in the UK Post Office study for an average of three interviews (Allinson et al., 1989). Even if the benefits seem small – months rather than weeks between periods of depression, 2 weeks more at work per year – then economically and personally they can be very worth-while.

Little is known about why counselling is effective. Radically different techniques seem to be equally success-ful. One explanation is in terms of common factors like support ('warm involvement') and challenge ('com-municating a new perspective on client or situation') (Stiles et al., 1986). Another possibility is that different approaches 'fit' different clients.

A final, major point about effectiveness is that it is very easy to believe that a particular method 'works' when it is irrelevant. This is partly because what we see and remember are open to bias, but also because many people (perhaps 40%) improve, or report they have improved, without counselling. If they had been in counselling they would probably have improved any-way, and inferred that the counsellor or technique was effective. This does not detract from the general conclu-sion that counselling helps people change more quickly and perhaps more substantially than no counselling.

For arguments against the effective-ness of most approaches to counsel-ling, see Eysenck (1992); you may also like to examine a re-analysis of the data in his original and stimulating attack (in 1952). McNeilly and Howard (1991) found a very substantial im-provement rate of 50% after about 15 sessions, compared to 2% in people not counselled, using the same data that Eysenck sees as demonstrating the ineffectiveness of counselling.

Barkham (1993a) provides practical guidelines for counsellors who wish to evaluate their own counselling and to make out a case for more resources.

EMOTIONS (*See also*: Collusion, Emo-tions (naming), Emotions (talking about versus experiencing), Empathy, Feelings, Paraphrasing, Process, Self-awareness, Thoughts)

The advantage of our emotions is that they lead us astray

Oscar Wilde

Most counselling and psychotherapy is based on the idea that we need to be aware of our emotions and feelings, and how they affect us. The difficult part is identifying and owning them. One obstacle is that emotions are often confused with thoughts. As a rule of thumb, emotions can usually come directly after the verb, e.g. I am happy; I feel sad. Exceptions include 'I feel thirsty' (a sensation) and 'I feel cheated' (which is a kind of emotion but one which people feel a variety of emotions about). However, when the word 'that' can be inserted after the verb, it is a thought, e.g. 'I feel all is lost', and 'I feel that all is lost'. The real emotion here remains unstated; it could be fear, anxiety or another emotion, we don't know. It is at this point that the counsellor may need to help clients become aware of the emotions underlying their statements and of the difference between thoughts and emotions.

Sometimes clients have great difficulty in expressing emotions, and counsellors may be unaware of this or even collude with it, because they too don't want to talk about the subject. One way of picking up unspoken emotion is by becoming aware of your own emotions. If there is a strong emotion or feeling around, checking it out with clients may increase their awareness of those feelings. An example of this was a trainee counsellor who in supervision complained of feeling hopeless and useless as the client had said very little. She was encouraged to check these emotions out with the client in the next session, who confirmed this was just how she (the client) felt. On the other hand, the much-used question 'how do you feel about that'? is often quite unhelpful, because the client is unsure. It also tends to make clients think, which takes them away from emotions and feelings. Instead, an empathic statement like 'you sound worried' may help clients awareness of their emotions.

Some counsellors find Greenberg and Safran's (1990) distinction between primary, secondary and instrumental emotions useful. Greenberg and Safran argue that it is only working with primary emotions that leads to change. Primary emotions are typically referred to as 'authentic' or 'real', while secondary emotions are a response to them or to thoughts, and ways of coping with rather than experiencing primary emotions. An example is being angry (secondary emotion in this case) as a reaction to feeling afraid (primary emotion here). To focus on your client's secondary emotion would in their view simply reinforce it, and not lead to change. In Greenberg and Safran's terms, instrumental emotions have been learned, and are used to influence or manipulate others. Generally, counsellors therefore need to challenge them (or help clients self-challenge). For example, some people have learned that if they get angry, people tend to give way.

Physiologically, emotions originate in the limbic system, an older part of the brain in evolutionary terms, and can be suppressed by activity in the cortex, or new brain. This means that by thinking we can suppress emotions, and that, conversely, by reducing cortical activity, e.g. by deep relaxation, we can allow emotions to rise (Mueller, 1983; Lancaster, 1991). Thus physiological understanding helps to clarify what is happening when for example a Gestalt counsellor asks a client to express emotions, or a Rational Emotive therapist suggests that a change in thinking will change emotions. Both are accessing the emotional system through speech, but have differing rationales about what will help the client and why.

EMOTIONS, NAMING (See also: Anger, Emotions, Empathy, Feelings, Literal description, Paraphrasing)

Table 4 is one way of helping clients find the right words by choosing the general category or categories first, then narrowing the search down. Or ten 'units', with a miscellaneous option, can be assigned, as in 'I'm 3 parts happy, 5 parts confused and 2 miscellaneous' (Green, 1964). Another method, which some clients find particularly helpful, is to try to 'ground' an emotion, sensation or thought in the person's body e.g. 'Where do you feel empty?' 'Can you describe your sense of empty?' Repetition by the client and repeating at a slower pace can also help clients to clarify.

The four category system assumes that there are basic emotions and that these four terms describe them. Both assumptions are disputed by researchers. Ortony and Turner (1990) for example argue that 'there is little agreement about how many emotions are basic, which emotions are basic,

and why they are basic' (p. 315). However nearly all the theorists agree on anger, sadness, fear and happiness. For a reply to Ortony and Turner, see Ekman (1992, 1993) who is particularly interested in those emotions which can be observed from facial expression, and in the high level of agreement across cultures in selecting emotion words that fit facial expressions. He also mentions the familiar idea to counsellors that people differ in their habitual 'affect-about-affect', e.g. some people are afraid of their anger, others disappointed in themselves for being angry, others disgusted, and so on (Ekman, 1993).

There is great similarity across different cultures about the categories of emotion (Russell, 1991). However, there are also emotion words in some languages with no English equivalent, e.g. Schadenfreude (German word for 'pleasure derived from someone else's displeasure'), and itoshii (Japanese word for 'longing for an absent loved one', though the English word 'pining' may come close) (Russell, 1991).

EMOTIONS, TALKING ABOUT VERSUS EXPERIENCING (See also: Empathy, Experiments, Immediacy, IPR, Paraphrasing, Self-awareness)

Emotions can be talked about in a distant unemotional way. In counselling, particularly, this is often not helpful and counsellors have many approaches for encouraging clients to 'make greater contact with' their emotions and experiencing them more clearly and deeply. They include asking the client to go through their reactions to an

Table 4 Four kinds of emotion,* with examples

Angry (*Mad*)		Sad	
High	*Medium*	*High*	*Medium*
Disgusted	Angry	Depressed	Discouraged
Furious	Exasperated	Defeated	Unhappy
Bitter	Frustrated	Devastated	Low
Seething	Miffed	Empty	Bruised
	Provoked	Worthless	Disappointed
	Sore	Hopeless	Hurt
	Annoyed	Crushed	Ashamed
	Fed-up	Battered	Upset
			Guilty
			Gloomy
			Fed-up

Afraid (*Bad*)		Glad	
High	*Medium*	*High*	*Medium*
Petrified	Anxious	Ecstatic	Pleased
Terrified	Insecure	Elated	Happy
Deeply shocked	Nervous	High	Cheerful
Horrified	Shaky	Delighted	Confident
Panicky	Cautious	Strong	Contented
Frozen	Unsure	Enchanted	Calm
	Muddled	Powerful	Affectionate
	Confused	Dynamic	Trusting
	Lost	Loving	Friendly
	Apprehensive	Devoted	Peaceful
	Threatened	Enthusiastic	Hopeful
	Vulnerable	Proud	Relieved
	Scared	Inspired	Interested
			Alert
			Determined
			Excited

*The subcategories of High and Medium intensity are very rough guides; what matters is that the client (or yourself) finds the right word or words, modified perhaps by 'very' or 'a bit'. A word like 'jealous' might be (i) helpful in its own right but also (ii) a combination of say, 'angry' and 'sad', so that, sometimes, words from these categories will be clearer still. Mad, sad, bad and glad are the terms used by Yalom (1989). As a group they have the advantage of resonance and therefore memorability, but two of them can be easily misinterpreted.

event more slowly; to repeat words or a gesture; to use the word 'I'; to say something louder, or in an exaggerated way; to exaggerate it yourself; to ask where and how something feels; immediacy; and two chair technique. It seems to be particularly helpful (in clarifying thoughts and wants as well as emotions, and making more sense of things) to experience emotions as they feel at that moment.

EMPATHY (*See also*: Core conditions, Counselling, Frames of reference, Metaphors, Paraphrasing, Stress)

Rogers (1980) defined empathy as follows: 'It means entering the private, perceptual world of the other and becoming thoroughly at home in it. It involves being sensitive, moment by moment, to the changing felt meanings which flow in this other person. ... It means temporarily living in the other's life, moving about in it delicately without making judgements; it means sensing meanings of which he or she is scarcely aware. ... It includes communicating your sensings of the person's world ... You are a confident companion to the person in his or her inner world. ... ' (p. 142). Most forms of counselling see empathy as a necessary quality of the effective counsellor.

Empathy is not sympathy or identification. Counsellors should guard against their responses being sympathetic *at the expense of being empathic*. Identification – where you feel a client's situation is similar to your own – can lead you to respond to your clients from your own experience rather than from within the client's frame of reference.

Empathy needs to be communicated to clients if they are to experience it directly. A good empathic response communicates an understanding of the content of the client's words, but more importantly, also captures some, at least, of the emotion that lies behind the words.

For example, a client says, 'I don't know what I feel towards my father. There are so many layers of feeling, some really deep, but one minute I seem to hate him, and the next to love him. I wish I could sort out what my real feelings are.'

If the counsellor responds, 'You just don't know what you feel', this would be accurate in part, but not very empathic.

If the counsellor responds, 'There are so many mixed feelings, you get really confused. But you would like to get clear what are the real and deep feelings you know are there somewhere', this would be more empathic because it responds both to the other person's confusion, and to their desire for clarity. In contrast, a question like 'can you say more about these feelings?', is not empathic, and unlikely to be as helpful. It also asks the client to do something which he or she has already said is difficult.

Barrett-Lennard (1993) stresses, as we have done, the 'aroused, active reaching out nature of empathic response' (p. 4) and suggests several 'channels': sensitive restatement; metaphor and imagery, both as reflections and when they form spontaneously and intuitively in the counsellor; some actions; and sometimes a question 'pops forward', which 'could not be asked – would not occur – without an empathic awareness of the other's experiencing' (p. 8). (See also Mearns and Thorne, 1988; Merry and Lusty, 1993.)

Levenson and Ruef (1992) discuss definitions and measures of empathy, emphasizing the inadequacies of self-report measures and discussing their provocative finding of a relationship between 'shared physiology' (i.e. autonomic response) in two people and accurate judgment of 'negative' emotions in one of them by the other.

EMPATHY: A SECOND EXAMPLE

The client says: 'When I took my new boyfriend home for the first time, it was quite a big risk for me. I thought about it for ages, but I thought I'd give my Mum the benefit of the doubt, but she went absolutely spare. I was so embarrassed, and I thought, why is she doing this? This is a big mistake. She doesn't trust me to know my own mind at all. I was furious.'

Response 1

mmhmm

Response 2

I guess you felt hurt and discounted after plucking up the courage to do this. It sounds like you gave it a chance, but got really badly let down, and you're just so very angry with her.

Response 3

How did your father take it?

Response 4

Has your mother always been like this with you?

Response 5

You thought about it for a bit, but you took him home anyway. Your Mum was upset about it, and this annoyed you.

Response 6

Is this the same kind of thing as before? Like when you were telling me that your mother always disapproved of your friends at school.

Response 1 has been wrongly described as 'empathic, showing understanding, and that I was with my client and listening', but it is *not* empathic.

Responses like 2 are by far the most empathic.

Responses like 3 have been described as 'an open question or probe inviting my client to explore the situation further', but are not empathic.

Responses like 4 have been described as 'trying to look for patterns', and are not empathic.

Responses like 5 (which has some content accuracy, but little empathy) have been described as 'empathic', with no awareness that the emotions have been diluted from 'absolutely spare' to 'upset' and from 'furious' to 'annoyed'.

Responses like 6 have been described as 'making links with things from the client's past which she has already mentioned', and again are not empathic.

EMPOWERMENT (*See also*: Abuse, Assertiveness, Endings, Power, Self-awareness, Theory)

Although the word 'empowerment' is something of a cliché, it refers to the important idea of client autonomy and responsibility. Counselling aims to increase these qualities. Power in this context means the ability to influence what happens to us; it is the opposite of feeling powerless, helpless, alienated or out of control. For discussion, see Hopson and Scally (1981, Chapter 3) who take a skills approach, and Nelson-Jones (1984) who uses personal responsibility as the central concept of an integrative model of counselling.

ENDINGS (*See also*: Contract, Duration)

Ending counselling with each client can be by default, as frequently happens, with the client failing to turn up or leaving a message about not wanting to continue, or, more satisfying from the counsellor's point of view, by design. You may negotiate at the start how long counselling will last and even specify the ending date. More usually, however, the idea of ending will be put forward by you or your client when it feels appropriate and negotiated at that time.

Peake *et al*. (1988) suggest that counsellors may find it helpful to reflect on three questions about ending, concerned with explicitness, flexibility and the client's needs.

1. **How explicit is the issue of ending?** The question is whether you should make use of the fact that counselling will end or give way to the temptation to let it pass without any mention, inwardly promising to deal with it when it

happens. Knowing that 'the end is near' can enhance motivation; it helps some clients to concentrate their efforts on making the best use of the time available. Similarly, it can work against the procrastination and resistance to change that can accompany a sense of counselling as open-ended and everlasting. The loss, whether it is real or symbolic, embodied in ending the counselling relationship can be a very potent force for positive change.

If you use ending to try to stimulate change the next question is when to raise it. At the beginning, many counsellors will have discussed client expectations of how long it may take and there may be at least some implicit understanding that it will be a matter of so many sessions or so many weeks, months or years. After that, unless there is an explicit time-limited contract, it would probably be premature to raise the issue until counselling is firmly underway and indeed some real sense of progress has been achieved. Some counsellors find it useful to remind clients some time during each session how many sessions have gone and how many remain.

2. **How rigid is the decision about ending?** There are several related questions here. Should counselling finish on the agreed date, or can it be allowed to continue if the client wants it to do so? How flexible should a counsellor be about ending and what are the ramifications? What circumstances justify

an extension? The answers to these questions depend on the nature of the counselling goals and of your philosophy and theoretical model.

Some counsellors favour a staggered ending, increasing the time between sessions towards the end of a contract. This seems an especially useful way to work towards ending with a client you have seen for a long time. Another option is to offer a follow-up session some 3–6 months after the counselling has ended. This can help to consolidate progress made.

3. **What are the needs of your client around ending?** Many clients experience little if any difficulty, seeing the end of counselling as an inevitable and natural event. This may be most likely when the counselling is relatively short term, where there wasn't a strong attachment, or where the focus was on problem management. However, other clients find ending very difficult. They feel they won't be able to cope without the counsellor, and ending may re-stimulate earlier painful experiences of loss and separation. You may need to help these clients cope with ending by talking through their existential or developmental needs, acknowledging their achievements and resources, and deciding on particular strategies.

SOME PRACTICAL SUGGESTIONS FOR ENDINGS

The aims of spending some time on ending are to help clients to sustain any changes they have made and to look forward to a new beginning. The following questions provide a flexible framework:

1. **How does the client feel about ending?** You may need to encourage clients to talk about ending. Sometimes it is helpful to reassure clients that ending can produce feelings of loss and that this is a normal and natural part of the process.

2. **What has been achieved?** The intention here is to consolidate learning by examining what changes have occurred. Further changes may be anticipated and it may be appropriate to review and celebrate the client's strengths and achievements.

3. **How has it been achieved?** This question is concerned with helping your clients identify the ways in which they themselves have contributed to or are responsible for what has been achieved and the positive aspects of their relationship with you. The client's account of what has happened is the best predictor of whether changes will last; if clients attribute responsibility for any gains to the counsellor then it may be difficult for them to sustain and build on any useful changes beyond the ending (Peake *et al.*, 1988, p. 227).

4. **What still needs to be achieved?** This question is about identifying unmet goals, relative weaknesses and aspects clients feel they still

want to develop. Many counsellors believe that a lot of learning and change goes on not only between counselling sessions, but after counselling has ended. It is useful here to examine your client's available resources and support network and other options for maintaining and developing the gains achieved in counselling.

5. **What may happen in the future?** You may wish to help clients look positively towards the future, while not ignoring the possibility that problems or symptoms may return. It may also be appropriate to anticipate stresses and 'rough spots', and ways of coping or trying to cope with them. Here it can be helpful to identify indications of the need to start counselling again. Typically people go in and out of counselling rather than having one continuous period. A good ending makes it more likely that clients have positive feelings about this prospect rather than feeling like a failure or seeing counselling as a waste of time.

6. **What has happened in counselling?** The intention here is to help clients evaluate their experience of counselling. It may also provide you with valuable feedback on your approach.

The framework outlined above focuses on the client. You may also wish to reflect on your own experience, to review what has been achieved and how, and to work through your own reactions to an ending.

ETHICAL DILEMMAS (*See also*: Boundaries, Codes of ethics, Appendix A)

Bond (1993a), as part of his review of ethical issues in counselling, suggests a six-step process for resolving or at least clarifying dilemmas:

1. Describe the ethical problem or dilemma briefly.
2. Ask whose dilemma it is. Bond suggests the useful general principle (with important exceptions) that the counsellor is responsible for the methods used and the client for the outcome.
3. Consider all available ethical principles and guidelines. Use Codes of Ethics, consider general ethical principles like Respect for Autonomy, Non-maleficence (the principle of causing least harm), Beneficence (achieving greatest good) and Justice, and possibly seek legal advice.
4. Identify all possible courses of action.
5. Select the best course of action.
6. Evaluate the outcome.

For useful examples and discussion, see Bond (1993a, pp. 190–201).

ETHNIC ORIGIN, *See* Multiculturalism

EUROPE, BEING A COUNSELLOR IN (*See also*: British Association for Counselling)

The European Association for Counselling (EAC) was registered in June 1993. Its aim is 'to develop an interactive view of counselling which approaches in a holistic way the special cultural, economic and emotional issues facing inhabitants in Europe.' Since the formation of EAC, other European countries have started to form national associations for counselling which, like BAC, support EAC.

BAC has a European Working Party to represent the interests of BAC members in European events. The European Association for Psychotherapy based in Vienna, and founded in 1991, is working with EAC. For more information, see van Deurzen Smith (1992).

EAC can be contacted c/o The British Association for Counselling (see separate entry).

European Association for
Psychotherapy
Maria Theresienstrasse 32–34/2/25
1010 Vienna
Austria.

Tel: 222/310 6408
Fax: 222/310 6409

EVALUATION, *See* Effectiveness

EXERCISES/ACTIVITIES, *See* Experiments

EXPECTATIONS, CLIENTS' (*See also*: Effectiveness, Common elements, Information)

Clients do not usually enter counselling in complete ignorance of what to expect, or of how counselling might help them. Some clients, however, have unreasonable or mistaken ideas about counselling. They, for example, expect to be given helpful advice or told how to overcome their problems. Others expect to *have* to talk about childhood memories, or to lie on a couch and be 'analysed'. See McLeod (1990) for a review of research on clients' experience of counselling and their expectations.

If you do an assessment interview, or contract-setting interview, you will be able to explore these expectations, and be clear with your clients what is expected of them, and what they can reasonably expect of you. Launching straight into counselling without exploring expectations can store up problems for later, particularly when clients feel disappointed or let down because they had unrealistic expectations to start with.

Reasonable (and common) expectations of clients include: confidentiality, the chance to be listened to, the possibility that painful memories or feelings may be stirred up, the probability that counselling will have a positive effect on their lives, that they will feel differently after counselling than they did before it, and that they will gain fresh insights and perspectives on themselves and their lives.

Unrealistic expectations include instant 'results', the solving of financial or social problems such as bad housing or unemployment, that they can change other people's behaviour, that the past can somehow be changed or that they will supply the problems and you will supply the solutions. People whose expectations are low or non-existent very rarely enter counselling voluntarily, and if they do, they tend to leave early. Clients with very high expectations may be disappointed when changes don't happen overnight, and may also leave counselling early. Other clients need time to adjust their expectations gradually; for them the process of induction is partly about learning what is realistic.

The degree of faith or belief the client has in the effectiveness of counselling is likely to influence how effective the counselling will be in reality. The fact that counselling exists at all, points to the notion that people do believe that change is both possible and desirable, and that it can be accomplished through a relationship with a skilled and trained counsellor. This expectation is supported by research (see entry on Effectiveness), and therefore it is a matter of being optimistic about the *possibilities* without exaggerating them.

EXPERIMENTS, BY CLIENTS (*See also*: Challenge, Counselling, Information)

The idea of inviting clients to try an experiment is a common strategy in co-counselling, Gestalt and some forms of behavioural counselling. For example, Gestalt two chair technique, which can seem a very strange thing to offer to clients, can be introduced in this way. 'There seem to be two parts of you arguing here, and going round and round, so that you feel exhausted and helpless. ... I'd like to suggest a kind of experiment to try and clarify the two sides. It means you sitting in this chair when you're arguing one way and in this chair for the other side. Would that be OK?'

If an experiment is approached in this way – as an invitation to try something and see what happens –

clients can reject the idea more easily. If they do, it may be useful to talk about what it is that the client finds difficult. The word 'experiment' has the drawback of sounding cold to some people, but it also suggests trying something out. 'Exercise' is sometimes accepted more readily.

Experiments can take place during counselling as well as between sessions, e.g. you might invite the client to pay attention to the way their arms are folded across their stomach, and to stay in that position, then perhaps to pull their arms in tighter and talk about how that feels. Alternatively, you might invite them to put their arms down by their sides and to talk about the difference. As an experiment outside the counselling session, you might invite your client to try to count to ten before saying anything the next time a particular situation occurs and to discuss whether the client was able to do it and what it felt like, in the next session. The beauty of an experiment is that it is just that – an experiment. If it is introduced sensitively, it can't go wrong, and it can help to change a client's familiar and distressing pattern of behaviour.

However, inviting a client to try an experiment is very different from a counsellor experimenting on a client. We regard this as unethical and potentially harmful. As a general rule, we strongly advise that you offer to clients only those experiments that have a clear purpose, and that you have experienced as a client or at least tried out in controlled training situations with colleagues.

F

FEAR, IN CLIENTS (*See also*: Anger, Emotions)

Fear is the response to a real or imagined threat. It is closely related to anxiety which is the prediction of fear, whether or not it is based on a previous frightening experience. Fear is shown by fight, flight, or 'freezing' behaviour in both animals and people. Fight is seen in angry clients, whose anger also may be shown by criticisms, or guilt as well as by shouting or fighting. Their behaviour or feelings are directed towards a target, possibly even themselves. Flight is exhibited in clients who avoid or deny, while people who freeze are more likely to suppress their feelings or be indecisive. Fear therefore may be behind many problems, from phobia and panics to depression and denial, criticism and paranoia.

Some approaches to counselling encourage clients to overcome fear by talking about and understanding it, while others emphasize action more. In all cases the client is in some way facing the fear, either by expressing it, or by finding ways of experiencing the fear-producing situation. These are not new ideas. For hundreds of years it has been known that if you fall off a horse for example, you need to get back on as soon as possible to overcome the fear and prevent it from growing. What we have not been aware of for so long is the wide range of conditions which result from fear. Fear can result from anything that is perceived as threatening, or from potential loss of control. There may be some obvious physical cause, but emotional abuse, where basic needs such as respect, love or attention are not met, can also cause fear, particularly in the very young (Rowe, 1987; Jeffers, 1991).

FEAR, IN COUNSELLORS (*See also*: Supervision)

From time to time counsellors, particularly trainees, may become fearful or anxious. They are then likely to become more concerned about what is going on for them than for the client. This can result in over- or under-reacting to the client or following your own ideas rather than what the client is saying. Such problems can usually be worked through in supervision, but if occurring often may indicate a need for personal counselling or training. See Dryden (1992a), Mearns (1990a, 1990b), Shohet and Wilmot (1991).

FEEDBACK FROM CLIENTS TO COUNSELLOR (*See also*: Challenge, Clients who don't come back, Drama triangle, Endings, Empowerment, Immediacy)

It is important that you remain open to receiving feedback from your clients, to help you check the extent to which you are enabling your clients to move towards more fulfilling or effective ways of living. In counselling sessions themselves, you will get feedback from your clients concerning the extent to which they feel understood and valued, both indirectly through comments like, 'Yes, that is how things feel at the moment', and directly – what clients actually say to you about their experience of you.

Whether or not the client continues to attend counselling with you is a form of feedback. It is possible, however, for clients to continue with counselling even though they don't seem to be deriving any benefit from it, or for clients to drop out for their own reasons, quite separate from counselling or you. Or you may have a client who is often late, or often wishes to leave early, or who misses

sessions regularly. They may be making an indirect statement about the counselling itself. It is usually helpful (and clear) to find a way of bringing this indirect form of communication out into the open, perhaps by sharing your feelings of concern about it.

The things clients say about their lives in general may contain important indirect feedback for you as a counsellor. For instance, someone who reports having a wider circle of friends and acquaintances than before is usually providing some positive feedback. Likewise, someone who reports more isolation from others may be providing useful feedback for you. Related forms of feedback concern, for example, how far your clients are able to speak about themselves and their feelings more directly than before, how far your clients seem to be less dependent on other people for their sense of self-esteem and how far your clients are becoming more proactive and 'in charge' of their lives. It is helpful to become sensitive to these kinds of 'clues' about how your client is making use of counselling, and, where appropriate, to incorporate them into the relationship you have with your client. However, it is important to interpret them cautiously; they may say more about the client or the client's need for a particular response from you than about you.

FEELINGS (*See also*: Emotions, Self-awareness, Support groups, Values)

Nichols and Jenkinson (1991) suggest that a feeling is more complicated than experiencing emotion. They define feeling as 'the current physiological and psychological stance of the person' and the general 'atmosphere' of your body, e.g. relaxed or fidgety, calm or restless (p. 45). 'Feeling' also refers to a way of making decisions, one which is based on values. Rogers' term 'organismic valuing process' has a similar meaning. Unfortunately, in practice, the terms 'feeling' and 'emotion' will probably continue to be confused, as will 'think', 'intuition', 'sense', and 'experience'.

FEES (*See also*: Boundaries, Contract, Information)

Apart from inviting clients to pay a donation – common practice in some agencies – there are three main ways of setting fees: (i) a fixed fee per session, and negotiating a lower fee in exceptional circumstances, (ii) a sliding scale, negotiating with each client an agreed point on that scale (for example a 50 minute counselling session for 1/40 of the client's income per week), and (iii) a fixed fee and not willing (or able) to work for anything less. In addition, some counsellors offer the initial interview free of charge, and part of this interview is concerned with agreeing about fees. An underlying principle which may appeal is that neither you nor your client feels exploited.

The options for when the fee is paid are payment for each session at the time, or payment in advance for a fixed number of sessions, or for you to invoice the client every month or so. If you choose the first option, you are likely to lose the fee for a missed session. If you choose the second option you need to discuss with your clients the consequences of missing sessions. A good way forward is to establish with your clients a minimum period of notice for missing sessions, after which the fee will not be refunded or carried over. Some counsellors ask for a set reduced fee for cancelled sessions. The same period of notice – typically not less than 24 hours – can apply to the counsellor postponing a session.

As a general guide, fees in 1993 ranged from £10 to £40 per session, with an average fee of £20 to £25. Not many counsellors in private practice can afford to have more than one or two clients at the lower end of this scale. Bartering (of services or goods) may be an attractive possibility, though maintaining boundaries is the primary consideration. Moreover, if your 'income' in this form is regular and can be defined by the Inland Revenue as coming from a business, then you may still be liable to tax on the monetary equivalent.

The Inland Revenue require accurate records of all payments made to you, and of all expenses incurred as a result of your practice. You may wish to consult an accountant about what expenditure can be offset against tax.

FINDING CLIENTS, *See* Advertising, Marketing

FIRST IMPRESSIONS (*See also*: Furniture, Self-awareness, Transference)

First impressions can have a disproportionate power. We tend to form them very quickly and almost automatically, then interpret later information in terms of them, i.e. to treat our first impression as accurate and any later information which conflicts with it as untypical. This is likely to lead to bias; accurate judgements are more likely if equal weight is given to equally important pieces of information, whether they come first or later. Good counsellors do this anyway: treating impressions (which are probably inevitable) as hypotheses but being ready to revise them. Intuitions are thus neither ignored nor believed, but checked.

Compelling first impressions are particularly likely to be wrong, because there hasn't been time to gather enough evidence and because their strength must come from something in you. Co-counselling refers to 're-stimulations' and suggests a procedure for dealing with them. A version of this is:

1. Ask 'Who does this client remind me of'? (It could be an actual person or a stereotype, e.g. a teacher).
2. In what ways? (Be as specific as possible and repeat the question after each response).
3. What do I want to say to this person? (What haven't I said that I want to?)
4. In what ways is this client *not* like this other person? (Again, repeat the question after each response).

Sometimes of course a client may be restimulated by you, and can use the same process.

Similarity is the strongest general source of bias in first (and later) impressions. We tend to like people who are like ourselves. Physical attractiveness is also potent; we tend to believe that 'what is beautiful is good'. To increase accuracy of judgement, it follows that counsellors need to know themselves, and to beware of these human tendencies. For discussions of research on forming impressions see Aronson (1992) and Nicolson and Bayne (1990).

FIRST SESSION, *See* Assessment, Beginnings, Clients, Contraindications, Defining counselling to clients, Contract, Difficulties in being a client, Expectations, Fees, First impressions, Furniture, History, Referral, Smoking

FOCUS, *See* Summaries, Counselling

FORCEFIELD ANALYSIS (*See also*: Counselling, Journal)

Force-field analysis is a standard technique for helping clients clarify a problem of decision (e.g. Egan, 1990). Parts of its value lies in actually writing things out, externalizing them instead of churning them around. Each arrow in Figure 1 represents either an

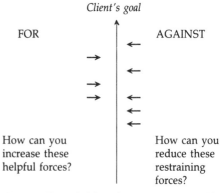

Figure 1 Force-field analysis.

obstacle or a positive force, and your client first explores each one and then, if appropriate, chooses some form of action. Suppose the problem is whether to get married or not, and one of the obstacles is your client's concept of marriage, in particular an underlying irrational belief about marriage. The action could be for him or her to replace the belief or to negotiate with the intended partner, or both. Or the obstacle may just become unimportant as your client explores it.

In more detail, a procedure is to work through the following steps:

1. First state the goal – what the client wants to achieve, avoiding either/or goals.
2. Generate a list of obstacles or forces against achieving the goal and a list of forces that contribute towards achieving it. The reasons why the client wants to achieve the goal may not always be a positive force. Be aware of the impact of each force. Not every positive force will have a corresponding negative force. It is important not to censor at this stage, but record ideas as they come.
3. Analyse the forces. Perhaps circle significant forces – those that are real and not assumed. Inadequate information may make this difficult and more information may have to be obtained. The forces on each side could be graded.
4. Identify ways to maximize the positive forces and minimize forces against achieving the goal. Focus on the most significant

forces. Again be specific and relate action to particular forces. Make a note of significant forces for which no action is possible.
5. Assess the feasibility of the stated goal. Does the action substantially offset the obstacles? Overall, do the positive forces outweigh the obstacles? If so go ahead. If not:
6. Forget or adapt the goal. The goal may be too general and not reflect the real problem. It may also contain more than one goal; if so, try to break it down further.

The analogy in force-field analysis is a warlike one, and the battle is between restraining forces, which might include guilt, irrational beliefs and practical problems, on one 'side', and positive forces, say a strong desire, a sense that things could be much better, some opportunities, on the other. Each force is explored and may lead to workable action, to either increase the positive forces or decrease the restraining ones.

FRAMES OF REFERENCE (*See also*: Boundaries, Challenge, Empathy, Paraphrasing)

'Frame of reference' is another way of expressing the idea of empathy. To stay within the client's frame of reference is to be empathic in a sustained way. An accurate paraphrase is, by definition, in the client's frame of reference. Conversely, in your own frame of reference, you see the client from your own viewpoint, e.g. 'It doesn't look that bad to me', or 'I don't think you're overweight'.

FRAMEWORKS (*See also*: Counselling, Theories)

Frameworks are working maps, to help counsellors make sense of or offer plausible explanations of aspects of clients, counselling and themselves. They therefore have the same purpose as theories and models, and indeed the three terms often seem to be used interchangeably. Some people seem to be drawn to very simple frameworks which they may then complicate when trying to understand a person or a process; others seem to be drawn to initial complexity which they then select from to clarify or 'get hold of' particular instances.

An example of a simple framework is 'Support and Challenge'. For many counsellors these two terms have proved to be a kind of life-line. More specifically, you can ask during a counselling session or later 'At this point am I supporting or challenging, and which do I want to be doing? And why?' A simple framework can quickly lead to quite complex considerations.

FREEWRITING (*See also*: Assertiveness, Journal, Self-awareness, Stress, Writing)

Freewriting is a way of exploring inner experience. It is also a technique for tackling writer's 'block'. There are three steps:

1. Write *without stopping* for several minutes (e.g. 10). If you are stuck, write something, e.g. 'I'm stuck' or 'I'm fed up with this stupid exercise', again and again if that's what comes to mind. Write anything but keep writing.
2. Underline significant bits and add any emotions.
3. Analyse, and consider whether any actions are suggested.

Freewriting thus replaces 'Think clearly and then write' with 'Write to find out what you mean, feel and want'. Essentially, writing and editing are separated with lots of writing and lots of discarding.

FREQUENCY OF SESSIONS (*See also*: Contraindications, Duration, Length)

In psychoanalysis, it is not unusual to see the same client three times a week, or even more, but most counsellors see clients only once a week. Once a week seems to be acceptable to most people (it is convenient and not too costly) but there is no real reason why it should be a 'golden rule'. For example, if a client is in a deeply anxious or very vulnerable state, it can help to meet more often than once a week, though most counsellors would see such an arrangement as temporary. It is probably better to have more frequent meetings in the early stages, and then to settle on once a week meetings later on, rather than the other way round. Rowan (1983) thinks it is more encouraging to reduce the frequency of meetings, and more anxiety-provoking to increase them.

After a while, some clients prefer to meet once a fortnight if they feel they have made a lot of progress and now only need support to consolidate the changes they feel they have made. Once a month may be too infrequent, and if a client asks for this we advise you to check out the reasons, and perhaps question whether or not they should leave counselling entirely. Once a month meetings may tend to become reports on what has happened since you last met, which is unlikely to be useful. Rowan (1983) advises the compromise of having a batch of weekly meetings, then a break of 2 or 3 months, followed by weekly meetings if necessary.

FRIENDSHIP/MAKING FRIENDS WITH CLIENTS (*See also*: Boundaries, Sexual attraction)

Counselling is a specific activity and its boundaries and limitations need to be respected and maintained. This is helpful and reassuring to both counsellors and clients. Sometimes clients do ask for a relationship outside counselling, but it is inadvisable to allow this, especially whilst counselling is continuing. You can explain that you can be of more help if the counselling relationship remains protected and uncomplicated by outside situations.

Once the counselling relationship is over, there are still problems with becoming socially involved with clients, at least until some time has elapsed. This does not have to be seen as an experience of rejection, but rather as a way of ensuring that you are available to help in the future, which might be impossible if you have become too close to the client. However, if you do become friends with ex-clients, and

this does sometimes happen, there will be no professional problem provided it is clear that you are no longer available as that person's counsellor.

FURNITURE (*See also*: Drinks/refreshments, Power, Tape-recorders)

Your furniture contributes to your clients' initial impression of you. If the impression is a negative one, you have to be correspondingly more effective to compensate. In part your choice of furniture depends on your approach to counselling (e.g. couch or not, cushions or not), but there are some general guidelines too. If you take the view that the disparity in power between counsellor and client should be reduced as much as possible then chairs and seating positions should be equal. Across the corner of a desk is the position sometimes used, though this is not equal: the counsellor, seated in front of the desk, can write on it more easily. Most counsellors prefer no desk.

Perhaps the most practical suggestions are to rôle-play being a client (i.e. in your own room), and to seek the views of colleagues and perhaps clients (near or at the end of their time with you). Some personal things and an intermediate degree of tidiness seem to be interpreted by most people as welcoming, but some counsellors prefer a plain room with no distracting objects. The balance sought may best be seen as one between neither deterring nor inhibiting clients – for example, family photos may discourage some clients – and being consistent with yourself and therefore more at ease.

G

GOOD COUNSELLORS (*See also*: Empathy, Genuineness, Psychological type, Respect)

Ideas about 'good counsellors' are usually expressed in terms of personal qualities of the counsellor, though, from the client's point of view, a good counsellor is one they like and feel comfortable with. Even if the 'match' between counsellor and client is the most potent factor, personal qualities are a necessary ingredient for effective counselling. Perhaps the most likely characteristics of good counsellors are the 'core qualities' emphasized in client or person-centred counselling: empathy, acceptance and genuineness. Brenner (1982) suggested five qualities; empathy, composure; readiness to discuss everything ('Open, precise communication about each topic that the client introduces – directly or indirectly – is the heart and soul of successful psychotherapy and counselling' (p. 7)); encouragement, or belief in the client's potential to function more fully; and purposefulness. Reddy (1987) also recognizes the core qualities and suggests others but adds, tartly, that 'Taken together these qualities seem more like a preparation for sainthood than for a job' (p. 43) and that a particularly necessary quality is 'freedom from the need for perfection' (p. 44).

Psychological type theory (e.g. Myers, 1980) suggests a different perspective on the idea of 'good counsellors': that each counsellor, depending on their psychological type, is likely to be most comfortable and effective in different schools, styles, stages and skills of counselling. For example, counsellors of one psychological type will tend to be more skilled at observing non-verbal cues than at detecting themes; counsellors of the opposite type will tend towards the reverse pattern. Similarly, counsellors who find support comes 'naturally' may find challenging more difficult, and vice versa. Again, some types are more comfortable with exploration (tending to neglect action), others more comfortable with action (tending to neglect exploration) (Bayne, 1993). However, there is a quite marked bias in counselling generally towards preferences for Feeling (dealing with people) and Intuition (inferring meanings). This does *not* mean that other types should avoid counselling: all the types can be good counsellors and clients, but with different patterns of strengths and comfort.

GROUP COUNSELLING (*See also*: Assertiveness, Referral, Self-awareness)

This is a very broad term covering all types of counselling for more than two people. There are many different ways of running groups, but the idea with most of them is that the members listen to, support and challenge each other. Members thus learn to be assertive and to experience how other people see them. The leader of the group may facilitate in a variety of ways. Some make process comments, others facilitate interactions between the members. Some clients find it useful to move from individual to group counselling as they gain confidence, others find the intimacy of one to one too threatening (Aveline and Dryden, 1988; Corey and Corey, 1992; Draucker, 1992, chapter 8; Rogers, 1973, 1980; Whitaker, 1985).

GUIDANCE

The concept of guidance was established in educational philosophy in the mid-1950s. It was an ambiguous term: some people saw it as meaning a more active-directed component of counselling, while others regarded counselling as an element of guidance. It is the latter definition that persists today.

Guidance is a generic helping strategy that encompasses a range of activities, of which counselling is one. Unlike counselling, the other activities are based on the helper's knowledge, skills and experience in a particular area. The four other guidance activities are:

- **Taking action** – speaking or taking some practical steps on behalf of the person being helped.
- **Advice giving** – making a suggestion based on personal evaluation or experience.
- **Information giving** – offering data, irrespective of any personal judgement of its worth.
- **Teaching** – imparting knowledge, attitudes and skills through structured experiences.

In common with counselling the aim of guidance is to promote self-reliance and enable the person being helped to cope more effectively with the presenting problem or issue. Bloch (1982) sees guidance as one possible intervention in crisis counselling work.

H

HIDDEN AGENDAS (*See also*: Collusion, Empathy, Immediacy, Manipulation)

Hidden agenda is the term used when somebody has a concealed purpose. By definition the person with this agenda knows that it is there, but tries to keep it hidden from others. For example, someone might come for counselling with a hidden agenda of just completing a required number of sessions without really looking at themselves, or someone in a group might be there because they are attracted to someone else in the group and are not interested in the group's overt agenda.

Hidden agendas can be quite disruptive, as it usually soon becomes apparent that things are not as they seem. Something is not right, but the reason is hard to discover. Empathy or immediacy may be the best ways of sorting out the impasse.

HISTORY TAKING (*See also*: Assessment, Working alliance)

A client history is a systematic collection of facts about the client's past and current life. Some counsellors do not take any form of client history as they feel that not only will much of the information be irrelevant, but that it may simulate the medical model in which clients, after responding to requests for information, may expect a diagnosis and a solution to their problem. Perhaps more importantly, the whole process of history taking can set up a relationship pattern which interferes with establishing an effective working alliance with the client. Attitudes vary with theoretical approach. For example, Adlerian counsellors may conduct a fairly long (i.e. over more than one or two sessions) lifestyle assessment inventory that is used for evaluation and diagnostic purposes (Dinkmeyer, 1985). This information, however, is gathered after an initial rapport has been established.

When an intake interview, sometimes called an initial assessment interview, is carried out, it is viewed as primarily informational rather than therapeutic. For this reason and/or because it is sometimes thought that an experienced or more senior person should be responsible for initial assessment and subsequent allocation to the most appropriate counsellor, it may be conducted by someone other than the counsellor who will work with the client. In other settings counsellors conduct their own intake interviews.

The purpose of a client history is to gather information about the client's background, especially as it may relate to current problems. A clinical history is not sought as an end in itself or because the counsellor will use it to structure the counselling or want to explore and focus on the client's history. Rather, it is used as part of the overall assessment process that may help the counsellor to understand the client's presenting problem. The assumption is that current problems are precipitated and maintained by events and experiences in the client's history.

Some counsellors prefer to collect some or all of the information in a brief questionnaire completed by the client. Others ask clients to write autobiographies, keep personal journals, write poetry or draw lifeline diagrams (time graphs in which key life points are marked along a time continuum), all of which can be used to supplement interview data.

POSSIBLE CONTENT AND SEQUENCE
(*See also*: Core qualities, Psychodiagnosis, Referral, Working alliance)

Cormier and Cormier (1991) identify the various kinds of information that can be obtained during a more formal history taking:

1. **Identification**. Name, address, telephone numbers, age, sex, ethnic origin/culture, marital status, occupation.
2. **General appearance**.
3. **Presenting problem(s)**. First occurrence, frequency, concurrent events; associated thoughts, feelings and behaviours, precipitating events, situations or people; previous ways of dealing with the problem; why counselling at present time.
4. **Previous counselling/psychiatric help**. Type, length, place of treatment; outcomes or reason for termination. Hospitalization and/or drugs for psychological problems.
5. **Education/Work**. Academic progress/attainment; relationships with peers/staff. Types and lengths of jobs; reasons for termination or change; further training, relationships with colleagues; most/least stressful and enjoyable aspects; current level of job satisfaction.
6. **Health**. Childhood diseases, illnesses, treatment received; current health-related problems, allergies, family health problems, sleep, eating and exercise patterns; typical diet, current medications.
7. **Social/Developmental**. Current lifestyle, economic situation, contact with people. Leisure interests. Religious affiliation. Values, priorities and beliefs. Earliest recollections; significant chronological events during main developmental stages.

8. **Family, marital and sexual.**
   - Details of mother, father and siblings. Quality of relationships, joint activities, parental rewards and punishments. Family psychiatric history.
   - Dating, engagement/marital/partnership history – reasons for termination.
   - Current relationship and sources of satisfaction/stress. Number and age of children.
   - Previous and first sexual experience, sexual preference, present sexual activity, frequency of intercourse, masturbation, current concerns/issues about sex.
9. **Communication style.** Verbal, non-verbal behaviour (voice, eye contact, body movements, personal space), and relationship behaviour.
10. **Diagnostic classification.** DSM III summary.

The last two categories are usually completed by the counsellor after the initial assessment or intake interview.

The sequence of obtaining this information in the interview is important. Generally, the interviewer begins with the least threatening topics and leaves the more sensitive areas until nearer the end of the session when there is likely to be a greater degree of rapport. The nature of the presenting problem will determine the extent and depth to which the areas are covered with each client.

HOLIDAYS

We suggest giving as much notice as you reasonably can to your clients when you plan to take a holiday, being as clear as you can about how long you will be away, and what arrangements need to be made for 're-entry' into counselling when you get back. If you will be away for long, your clients may like you to arrange for them to see a colleague meanwhile. A phone number where they can contact someone else is also helpful.

HOMEWORK (*See also*: Books, Brainstorming, Experiments, Journal, Life Space Diagram, Psychological type, Thoughts)

The term homework refers to specific activities clients undertake to complete between counselling sessions. Some counsellors prefer to call these activities tasks, assignments, practice or work between sessions (Dryden and Feltham, 1992). Homework is an integral feature of cognitive behavioural approaches to counselling and in particular, the brief therapies. It is not, however, exclusive to these approaches, and can encourage clients to recognize their own ability to initiate change, and to make connections between counselling and the rest of their lives. Trying out new behaviours may also consolidate learning and reinforce commitment to change. The various types of homework are listed below:

- **Reading** The client may be invited to read about some aspect of counselling theory or about someone else's experience and ways of dealing with their problem.

- **Writing** This may be anything from a very simple account of what the client wants from counselling, a journal style description of a particular situation or experience, to a full life story. Writing may also take the form of lists; of things to do, of issues or problems, of things the client is afraid of or anxious about. Making lists may also be a way of generating ideas or brainstorming ways of coping more effectively with a problem. Another form of writing is a letter to or from a real or imagined person. The intention of writing a letter to a real person is invariably not that it should be actually sent to that person, but as a vehicle for exploration or catharsis. Other forms of writing can be found in Rainer (1978).
- **Diagrams** Clients might prepare life space diagrams or genograms.
- **Questionnaires** These might include completing self-descriptive checklists, evaluation questionnaires, or inventories designed to elicit specific information, e.g. Psychological Type, Anxiety or Depression Inventories.
- **Recording** This is a written form of monitoring the occurrence of particular situations, feelings or behaviours. It may be done by keeping a diary or daily log.
- **Practical exercises** These may involve the client in trying out some new or different activity or behaviour, such as doing some kind of physical exercise, being more assertive in a particular way, initiating a dialogue with a particular person or implementing some rehearsed action to interrupt negative self-talk or obsessive behaviour. It may also involve the use of relaxation exercises.
- **Creative exercises** This may involve writing short poems, drawing or painting pictures or collages of special significance to the client. These are brought to a session and explored with the counsellor. Some clients may be able to use guided imagery and visualization rehearsed during the session.

GUIDELINES

The following guidelines are adapted from Dryden and Feltham (1992, 114–34);

- Explain the rationale behind any task.
- Avoid appearing to 'set homework': negotiate, and encourage the client to offer alternative ideas and modifications.
- Make sure that the task relates directly to the client's problem.
- Listen for and challenge any ambivalence and encourage commitment.
- Take the client's ability and circumstances into account.
- Discuss when, where and how the client will attempt the task.
- Establish with the client the criteria for evaluating the outcome.
- Explore any possible obstacles.
- Help clients to prepare by mentally rehearsing what they are going to do.

- Emphasize that whether clients feel they do it well or badly or don't actually do it at all, something valuable is likely to be gained from discussing their experience.
- Before the end of the session check that clients really do understand what to do and why they are doing it.

The next session

- It is essential to follow-up the task.
- Discuss what has happened.
- Discuss any reasons for not attempting the task.
- Explore what happened if the task was attempted, but not completed.
- Invite clients to take increasing responsibility for setting up their own tasks.

Dryden and Feltham also advise that counsellors might well learn how to help clients with homework assignments by first setting some for themselves!

HOOKED (*See also*: Drama Triangle, Emotions, Patterns, Process, Transference)

This rather jargonistic term is used in an interactive sense when the 'process' of one person catches – or hooks into – the process of another person. This is most clearly seen in the Drama Triangle, or in very emotional interactions when the emotion aroused seems out of proportion to the incident. It is also sustained in a compulsive way. For example if someone is in a Victim role, others try to do too much for them, or else get angry with them, thus getting hooked into their process. If you avoid being hooked, you can encourage the other person to develop their own sense of worth and self-esteem, and to free themselves, at least to some extent, from their self-defeating pattern.

HOSPITALIZATION, *See* Contraindications, Referral

HUMOUR (*See also*: Challenge, Empathy, Immediacy)

Clients who use a lot of humour, who try to 'entertain' you, who laugh too much at difficult situations, or make too many jokes about themselves and their experiences, may be communicating an inability or reluctance to face difficult circumstances openly. We suggest treating excessive displays of humour, or hostile humour, with caution. You may need to confront or challenge your clients with their behaviour, and explore what it might mean for them. This does not, of course, mean that every joke or laugh need be treated as a 'cover up'.

Using humour as a counsellor can be useful to offer a new perspective – seeing the absurd aspect of something and thereby gaining some control over it. However, as with everything else, too much or inappropriate humour can deflect the client from exploring difficult or painful experiences.

HUNCHES, *See* Challenge, Intuition

I

ILLNESS/DISABILITY, *See* Multi-culturalism

IMMEDIACY (*See also*: Assertiveness, Challenge, Self-awareness)

Immediacy can be defined as 'direct, mutual talk', for example 'I see us as going round in circles and I'm confused. I wonder if you feel the same way'. The following checklist defines immediacy in more detail and can be used for feedback. It is a set of guidelines rather than a prescription.

In your use of immediacy, did you . . .

- give some indication that you wanted to talk about the relationship between you;
- describe (rather than evaluate);
- 'own' it by using personal pronouns (I, my);
- use the present tense, emphasize the 'here and now' (e.g. At this moment I feel . . .);
- say something about (i) how you felt, (ii) how you sensed the other person was feeling, (iii) what you thought was happening between you and (iv) how you thought it was affecting what you were trying to achieve together;
- have a sufficiently strong relationship with your client;
- ask for your client's view.

For discussion, see Cormier and Cormier (1991).

INFORMATION, GIVING (*See also*: Advice, Challenge, Jargon, Process)

There is some confusion about the difference between giving information and giving advice. We suggest that information is intended to help the client decide for themselves, whereas advice tells the client the best thing to do. There is also a disagreement among counsellors as to whether giving information is appropriate. On the one hand, some counsellors give information because they believe it helps clients to understand themselves better and make decisions. On the other hand, there is the view that counsellors should never give information, usually on the grounds that clients will tend to construe it as advice because the counsellor is in a position of power. They may also blame the counsellor for any wrong decisions they take. Other counsellors think that giving information interferes with clients doing things for themselves.

Some types of information-giving (in the sense defined above) are:

1. **Challenge**, e.g. 'I have heard you call yourself silly on three different occasions'.
2. **Reply to a request for feedback**, e.g. when the client asks 'Do other people behave like me?' Sometimes it is appropriate to ask the client to check out for themselves whether this is so, or to ask *them* to try to answer the question. At other times it may be appropriate to say 'yes, they do and there are many different ways of behaving'.
3. **Enlarging the field of knowledge**, e.g. informing a bereaved client about the different stages of loss, and the wide variability in experiencing them or not.
4. **Helping clients to get information**, e.g. letting them know of a relevant book to read, or of an organization that could help them.

GUIDELINES

1. Is it of use to the client?
2. Check whether the client understands it.

3. Only give what seems to be needed.
4. Consider asking what, if anything, the client may do with the information.

Ley's (1988) recommendations include:

- find out what the person wants to know;
- check for jargon;
- use short words and sentences;
- be specific;
- categorize;
- summarize;
- check understanding (p. 179).

INSURANCE, INDEMNITY (*See also*: Sued (being))

The BAC Code of Ethics and Practice for Counsellors states that 'Counsellors should be encouraged to review periodically their need for professional indemnity insurance and to take out such a policy when appropriate'. This entry takes first the current 'official' view, as implied in this quotation, and then summarizes Mearns' (1993) forceful counter-arguments.

Indemnity insurance policies offer indemnity for liability at law for damages – claimants costs and expenses in respect of claims for breach of professional duties made against a counsellor as a result of alleged neglect, error or omission in the provision of counselling services. Some policies also provide cover for potential liabilities incurred outside the counsellor–client relationship, including approved research projects, teaching or seminars and written reports.

However, most policies have listed exclusions from legal liability which it is advisable to read through carefully. Murray (1992, R.4) suggests that there is always a discrepancy between what a practitioner thinks is covered, and the problems that an insurance company is willing to accept as valid claims under the policy. The level of indemnity may vary from £1000 to £500 000 and is determined by the premium you pay. Murray (1992, R.3) suggests that you need to consider what is the probability that during the next 12 months you will need to pay legal fees and expenses for problems covered by the policy. It would also be helpful to know the average amount of payments made. Murray acknowledges that insurance companies may be reluctant to give such information as it may reduce their sales!

With reference to the PPS Economy Scheme which Murray runs, he anticipated that claims and damages not exceeding £10 000 could be expected to occur with a frequency of around one in 10 000 practitioners a year. Counsellors who work within the NHS or in schools or colleges may find it useful to check whether they have indemnity cover from their authority or organization. This may depend upon whether they have 'counselling' specifically mentioned in their contract of employment. It often isn't.

THE CASE AGAINST

Mearns (1993) first points out that so far there have been no significant claims in Great Britain against professional malpractice, negligence, errors or omissions. The key concept (see entry on being sued) is 'reasonable behaviour'. However, he has other, less obvious reasons for regarding indemnity insurance 'with considerable derision':

1. If insurance exists, claims are more likely.
2. As a consequence of (1), insurers tend to advise not saying you are insured or admitting responsibility, which is dishonest.
3. Indemnity insurance assumes that counsellors are *responsible for* their clients (as a medical practitioner is for a patient), rather than responsible *to* their clients.

INTEGRATION AND ECLECTICISM
(*See also*: Common factors, Counselling)

'Integration' and 'eclecticism' are both defined in several different ways (Dryden and Norcross, 1990). In very broad terms, eclectic counsellors borrow the 'best' techniques and ideas from a variety of sources, and may do so haphazardly or systematically, while integrative counsellors try to form a coherent, harmonious whole from two or more theories or parts of theories.

As with the multicultural approach, it seems likely that it is desirable for counsellors to reflect on the various possibilities, find one or more that fits, and to re-consider from time to time. There is plenty of material to reflect on: Norcross and Grencavage (1989), in their introduction to a symposium on integration etc., identified 50 books 'on synthesizing various counselling concepts and theories', and there are of course many different, or apparently different, approaches to counselling (over 400 at the last count).

INTERPERSONAL PROCESS RECALL (IPR) (*See also*: Assertiveness, Process, Self-awareness, Supervision)

Interpersonal Process Recall (IPR) involves playing back a video or audio tape recording of an interaction, e.g. between you and a client. The purpose is to help participants recall what was happening in the original interaction: thoughts, emotions, feelings, images, body sensations, perceptions and expectations. The aim is self exploration and the development of interpersonal skills. IPR has been used in research, counsellor skills training, clinical supervision, especially reciprocal peer supervision, and the development of consultation skills.

IPR is primarily concerned with covert processes and what may be on the edge of the participants awareness. Kagan (1984) argues that people perceive much more about each other's communications and behaviour than they acknowledge to themselves or to the other person. Barker (1985, p. 155) encapsulates the underlying assumption when he states that 'accompanying even apparently trivial dialogue there seems to be an enormous breadth and depth of thoughts, feeling and fantasies – often of a surprisingly primitive nature – that are often quickly forgotten or suppressed'. For the counsellor, IPR is a way of what Barker describes as 'recapturing this internal stream of consciousness'. It is this potential wealth of information that counsellors may fail to acknowledge or use productively in the session with a client.

Kagan (1984) tells the story that in 1982 his University was at that time one of the few with professional video recording equipment. It was used to record eminent speakers to preserve their lectures for future use. The visitors were often curious and after their presentation asked to see and hear themselves in action. They were amazed at the detail and extent to which the recordings were able to stimulate their recall of the experience. They frequently remarked on discrepancies between how they remembered feeling at the time and how they appeared, and what they actually said and did at a particular moment. Kagan explained that as they were eminent speakers he felt only able to make respectful inquiries and encourage them to elaborate rather than offer any feedback or evaluation as he might have done with students. This became a crucial feature of IPR.

IPR was developed by Kagan within a primarily humanistic orientation and it seems compatible with any orientation that accepts the value of reflecting on inner experience. Furthermore, the specified questions or leads used in the Inquirer role (see next entry) are very useful additions to the counsellors repertoire of skills.

IPR AND THE INQUIRER ROLE

The process of recall is facilitated by a neutral third party, someone who was not involved in the original interaction. This person is known as the Inquirer. While listening to the playback the Inquirer waits until the person reviewing decides to stop the tape. Then, by using a series of highly probing but non-interpretive, neutral questions she or he invites them to recall, clarify and explore their experience more deeply. A central feature of IPR is that the control over when and where to stop the tape, and over how far the exploration should go, lies entirely with the recaller. In this way people review their own tape, retain the power within the recall situation and are responsible for their own self-discovery and learning.

The Inquirer role is easier to conceptualize than to actually do. It requires non-judgemental but assertive probing and consists entirely of asking brief, open-ended exploratory questions. The Inquirer assumes that the participants are the best authority on their own inner self-awareness and will choose to respond to or reject any of the questions offered. She or he also recognizes that the participant may not be able or not want to take up some of the questions. That is fine. The task is to facilitate the participant's own self-discovery and not to be drawn into counselling, 'active listening', giving information or even sharing observations.

Participants are helped to explore three dimensions of the interaction recorded on tape: what was going on within the participant, what was going on within the other person and what was going on between them. The focus is on the participant's reaction

'then', at the point at which the tape was stopped rather than the 'now' within the recall session. The questions seek to help the participant recall 'inside' thoughts etc. rather than specific behaviours. Some of the indicative questions from Kagan's checklist of 'often used Inquirer Leads', include:

- What were you thinking at that moment?
- What were you feeling?
- What pictures or memories went through your mind?
- What did you think the other person was feeling?
- What did you want the other person to think or feel?
- Was there anything you wanted to say but couldn't find appropriate words for?
- Did you have any physical sensations then? Where in your body did you most feel the impact?
- What had you hoped would happen next?
- Had you any goals or intentions at this point?

Other leads invite the recaller to take their initial response more deeply, exploring mutual perceptions and whether there was any special meaning or possible associations:

- What prevented you from saying what you really wanted to say?
- What effect did that perception have on you?
- How do you think the other person was feeling/thinking about you?
- Do you think s/he was aware of your feelings?

- What do you think s/he wanted you to think, feel or do?
- Do you think your description of the interaction would be the same as the other person's?
- Does that feeling have any special meaning for you? It is familiar?
- Does s/he remind you of anyone else in your life?

Before returning to the tape playback, the Inquirer typically checks out if there were any other thoughts or feelings around at that point. At the end of a recall session inquirer leads might include:

- Did the setting affect you?
- How did you feel about your own behaviour?
- If you had it to do over again, what if anything would you do differently?
- What things have you learnt from this recall?

IPR can uncover clinically important aspects of an experience, helping counsellors to become conscious of messages they denied or ignored, of previously unverbalized fears and imagined vulnerabilities or of when the client says something that makes them feel uncomfortable and that touches their own problems or defences. IPR can help counsellors develop their own internal supervisor and become more aware of the ways in which their covert experience within the interaction with their clients may have influenced or determined their behaviour – what they said or didn't say or do.

IPR INVOLVING THE CLIENT

The most obvious application of IPR within counsellor training or supervision is for counsellors to use an audio or video recording to recall their experience of working with a client, as soon as possible after the session. It can also be valuable if *clients* are invited to recall their experience. With the prior permission of the client or person in the client's role, this recall session is recorded and then used by the counsellor to learn about the client's perceptions and experience of the counsellor's behaviour and interventions. Alternatively, the Inquirer could report back to the counsellor.

A further variation is mutual recall, when both the counsellor and the client participate in the same recall session with an Inquirer. They are both asked to share their recalled thoughts and feelings, paying attention to how they perceived each other and what meanings they attribute to each other's behaviour. This is the most difficult form of IPR. Like the skill of immediacy it requires self-awareness, empathy, sensitivity to the other person and courage or assertiveness to share their experience and reaction to the other person. In counsellor and client recall, participants develop the ability to talk openly and non-defensively about the ongoing process between counsellor and client. Counsellors learn experientially about their own interpersonal impact, how they come across to others and the ways in which a client's concern may actually involve them. In mutual recall they learn to verbalize these processes in the relationship and to deal directly and explicitly with the relationship itself.

INTERPRETATION, *See* Challenge

INTUITION (*See also*: Boredom, Challenge, First impressions, Self-awareness)

Counsellors often talk of working by intuition, while trainers may encourage students to develop, follow (or at least take note of) their intuition. Some writers have gone as far as concluding that psychotherapy is as much a question of intuition as science, while others say that intuition does not really exist and it is 'merely a matter of subliminal, unconscious, or highly experienced reaction'. To mystics the intuitive is the level above the physical, emotional and mental. In the psychodynamic approach, 'free flowing attention' is letting your mind wander with the client's words in an open, wondering 'frame of mind'; in most approaches there is scope for sometimes tentatively expressing some of the images, thoughts or feelings (all intuitions) which then appear.

Whatever intuition is, there seems to be some agreement that it is enhanced when one is forced to act quickly without thinking, and that it occurs more when a person is relaxed, or thinking about something different. Conversely, when you are problem-solving, thinking, or feeling anxious, intuition is reduced, while emotionality and subjective involvement also interferes with it (Lancaster, 1991). All this implies that we are dealing with a phenomenon that is different from thinking, has little to do with the action of the cortex and is probably actively impaired by thought and logic. As counsellors are encouraged to be relaxed, empathic and to stay with the client's frame of reference rather than their own, this would seem to be a good state for intuition to develop.

Some counsellors describe their approach as 'intuitive'. We see it as important that, at least on reflection, they are able to account for what they do and why.

J

JARGON (*See also*: Information)

Jargon can be defined either as 'gibberish' or as 'language peculiar, and often useful to, a particular profession or group'. To an outsider, in this case someone unfamiliar with counselling language, these two things are indistinguishable. The point here is to avoid the use of jargon during your sessions with your clients. Using words like 'resistance', 'transference', 'empathy' and 'congruence' can be mystifying and alienating. In a similar vein, you may wish to avoid using clichés or 'counsellor speak' when counselling. Phrases like 'What I hear you saying is . . . ', or 'It sounds to me like . . . ' can become intensely irritating if used too often. If you regularly tape-record some of your sessions, you can look out for words or phrases that sound clichéd or repetitive.

JOURNAL, WRITING A (*See also*: Counselling, Freewriting, Self-awareness, Stress)

Rainer (1978) sees a journal as 'a practical psychological tool that enables you to express feelings without inhibition, recognize and alter self-defeating habits of mind, and come to know and accept that self which is you' (p. 18). It can help you discover genuine interests, nourish you, clarify goals, free intuition, and record insights. This kind of journal is therefore very like good counselling in its purpose and also its methods.

There are many approaches to writing a journal, including 'games you can play with your inner consciousness to get to know it better' (Rainer, 1978, p. 26). Some examples from Rainer (1978) and Adams (1990):

1. Lists e.g. of desires, things you feel uneasy about, things you're happy about, beliefs you've discarded, loves.
2. 'Portraits', e.g. describe a friend.
3. Describe a day.
4. At the end of a day, write one adjective to describe it and another to describe how you'd like the next day to be.

5. Freewriting: writing quickly and without stopping or editing.
6. Sitting quietly for a few moments before writing (to allow the most important incidents and feelings to begin to surface).
7. Writing with your other hand (the idea is to improve contact with emotions).
8. Writing about yourself in the third person.
9. Writing dialogues – with someone else; between part of you and another part of you.

A series of studies by Pennebaker and others (e.g. Pennebaker *et al.*, 1990; Pennebaker, 1993) provides strong evidence for the value of writing about troubling experiences (and indirectly for counselling). In one study, first-year students wrote continuously for 15–20 minutes on three consecutive days on their 'deepest feelings and thoughts' about coming to college. A control group wrote about what they'd done that morning, and were asked to be 'objective', i.e. not to mention emotions, feelings, or opinions. In line with previous findings showing improved functioning of the immune system, the first group visited the health centre less often in the following months than the control group.

Interview data supported an insight rather than a catharsis view of the more effective coping which seemed to come from personal writing (Pennebaker *et al.*, 1990). Alternatively, both processes might be at work but in different ways (Pennebaker, 1993).

In a pilot study summarized by Pennebaker (1993), participants were asked to write about their deepest feelings and thoughts each day for 2 weeks. On two of the days, they were given some words to include, e.g. 'negative' emotions, insight words like 'realize' and causation words like 'because'. They reported that these days were the least personal, most difficult to do, but also the most meaningful. In another study, without provided words, it was found that the participants who benefited most were those who used low rates of cognitive words on their first day of writing compared with their last (Pennebaker, 1993), i.e. they explored emotions first, before insights and ideas.

Pennebaker *et al.* (1990) argue (i) that not talking (or writing) about upsetting experiences is stressful because there is a basic need to talk about them which is actively inhibited, and (ii) that translating them into language helps the person clarify and think them through. Writing is of course much cheaper than counselling, more private, and more under the person's control, and it has a long history (Freud and Horney both wrote about self-analysis). However, this is not to say that self-analysis makes counselling redundant.

A general mode of counselling is clear in both Pennebaker's and Rainer's discussions: first, express and feel the problem fully, and second, analyse and think it through. Like counselling, this process aims to reduce confusion, clarify emotions, feelings, wishes, values and thoughts, and therefore free us to act more in the present.

For guidelines on a structured approach to writing a journal, with a 'worked' example, see Nicolson and Bayne (1990, pp. 54–56).

JOURNALS, ACADEMIC (*See also*: Research)

The leading UK journals for coun-sellors are *The British Journal of Guidance and Counselling* and *Counselling*. There are also occasional, excellent articles in several psychology journals. For examples of our choices see the references for this book. Titles and addresses of major counselling journals are listed in Appendix A.

K

KISSING (*See also*: Boundaries, Touch)

Counsellors often find issues to do with physical contact with clients problematic. In some forms of counselling, any physical contact, even shaking hands, is thought ill-advised. In humanistic counselling, a more relaxed attitude is taken, and touching and hugging do sometimes occur in counselling sessions or as a greeting or farewell.

In some cultures, including some European ones, kissing as a greeting or as a farewell is a ritual that need not have any special (i.e. sexual) significance, but even so, this form of physical contact usually only happens when people have known each other for some time. Our culture is not a homogeneous one, and different cultural groups have very different attitudes to kissing. Some find it very offensive while for others it is a normal ritual. Amongst some Europeans, kissing only *appears* to happen, there is no actual physical contact. And even if your culture expects or accepts 'ritual kissing', it may not be true of your client.

The real danger here is that a kiss can be misinterpreted, or invested with more significance than it really has. Even when you feel you know your client very well, and have enjoyed a long relationship, it may therefore be best to be very careful about how much physical contact, even of a ritualized kind, you allow. If problems do arise they can, of course, be talked through, and if you or your client has made a mistake this can be accepted and explored just like any other incident in counselling.

L

LENGTH OF SESSIONS (*See also*: Boundaries, Contract, Duration, Time boundaries)

Traditionally, sessions are 50 minutes long, and most counsellors have sessions of 50 minutes or an hour. The '50-minute hour' gives you a 10-minute break between clients if you have a full day of counselling, but most counsellors don't have practices that are as tightly organized as this, and some humanistic forms of counselling, particularly those involving a lot of body work, tend to work best in sessions of 1½–3 hours, or even all day. Mearns and a client hired a cottage for a week (Mearns, 1992, p. 75). Most counsellors and clients, however, seem to find 50-minute or one-hour sessions about right.

It is important to be clear with your clients very early on (probably in your initial interview) about the length of sessions, and to stick to your agreement – neither letting sessions drift past the agreed time nor finishing early. If clients are late for sessions, they shouldn't expect to be able to carry on past their allotted time other than in very exceptional circumstances. The way you use time is part of the way you protect boundaries in your counselling practice, and learning to use time effectively is part of what some clients need from their counselling.

LIABILITY AND THE LAW, *See* Insurance (indemnity), Sued (being)

LIFE SPACE DIAGRAM (*See also*: Emotions, Experiments, Life Space Exercise (using stones), Questions)

The Life Space Diagram is a method of helping someone explore and clarify their relationships with others. One advantage is its immediate visual impact, another its flexibility. Several steps are suggested:

1. Briefly describe the purpose of the exercise and invite the client to try it as a kind of experiment.

2. On a large piece of paper, although A4 size would be adequate, make a list of all the people who in one way or another have real significance in the client's life. Some clients feel uncomfortable about writing while someone is watching. If so, it is a good idea for you to offer to do the writing, following the client's instructions, checking whether or not you are doing it correctly. Another practical point is that some clients equate significance with positive or friendly, or people with whom they have frequent contact. It may be necessary to explain that people they dislike, who they hardly ever see or who are dead can still be significant for them, and therefore can be included in the Diagram.

3. Print the word ME to represent the client in a small circle in the centre of the page.

4. Consider each person from the list in turn, placing them as near to, even actually touching, or as far from, the ME as the client wants. Each has their own circle. The relative distance of each person from ME may represent the importance, closeness or intensity of feelings the client has towards them. The client decides what the distance or space means. The visual impact can be heightened by joining the other circles to the ME with a broken or continuous line of varying thickness. This may add some meaning for the client. A thick heavy line may represent a particularly strong attachment, whereas a broken line

may represent someone who is no longer alive, yet may still feel close to them and occupy their thoughts and feelings. It is important that the client decides the order and who to include or leave out. This in itself may be worth exploring with the client.

As each person is added to the diagram, you can encourage the client to talk about the relationship they have with that person, e.g. by asking:

• What do you think or feel about this person?
• What do you want or expect from them?
• What do you imagine they think or feel about you?
• What do you imagine they want or expect from you?

In a diagram which doesn't involve many people, a summary of the main thoughts or feelings could be written next to the appropriate circle.

As the Life Space Diagram nears completion you can stimulate further exploration and discussion with a series of prompts, appropriate for the client and presenting problem. For example:

• As you added new people did you want to move others nearer or further away from you?
• Is your relationship with anyone changing? Are they moving closer or further away from you? What is happening between you at the present time?
• What might the diagram have looked like a month, a year or several years ago? What has

caused any changes? What do you think it might look like in the future?

- How exact have you been in placing family and friends? Are they or should they be together in groups or more spread out, when you look at it carefully?
- Do you rely on certain kinds of relationships, e.g. friendship or work relationships? Does authority or power play a part in any of the relationships? What effect does this have?
- How do you feel about the way you are surrounded by your relationships? Is it a comfortable picture? How far is it a self-portrait? How would you like it to be different? What would you like to change? Can you see how you might take a step towards achieving any of those changes?

Some clients feel really good about what their Life Space Diagram represents for them. They may have many people touching the ME and have had difficulty getting everybody they wanted close enough to them. However, for other clients the exercise causes great pain and distress. When they look at their diagram they see in concrete visual form what at some level they know, but have not wanted or been able to admit. The diagram may include very few people with none touching ME and all spaced together around the edge of the paper. The empty space around the ME is seen and felt. It is important to be sensitive to the client's feelings and not to under-estimate the power of this exercise.

LIFE SPACE EXERCISE, USING STONES (See also: Counselling, Emotions, Life Space Diagram, Questions)

An alternative form of the Life Space Diagram uses small stones. The next time you go to the beach make a collection of pebbles of different shapes, sizes, textures and colours. You may like to have them in your counselling room in a large shallow wooden bowl. (It makes an attractive decoration too!)

The exercise is approached in much the same way as the Life Space Diagram except that instead of drawing names on a sheet on paper, pebbles are used to represent the people. You start by inviting the client to select a pebble to represent him/herself. The pebble is placed in the centre of a piece of white paper or cloth and then other stones are positioned around the client's own stone to represent his/her life space. Each stone is carefully selected so that in some way it represents the particular person. The size, shape or colour of the pebble may be given a particular symbolic meaning by the client. You can encourage the client to talk about why they chose each stone: The colourful and attractive personality. The big and strong personality. The small and dull personality. The beautifully rounded yet flawed personality.

The advantage of using stones or pebbles is that they can be held; their smoothness, roughness, size and shape, provides a potent kinetic experience. They can also be moved about to change or adjust their position in relationship with others as new 'people' are added. Although the purpose and approach to the exercise is very similar to drawing a Life Space Diagram, the experience for the client can be very different. There are obviously many variations to this exercise, e.g. using different objects. What is most important is that you recognize the potential impact of the exercise and allow plenty of time for it. The exercise is complete when the client wants to stop or has little to say. Although the exercise is usually part of the first phase of counselling, it can only be safely done when you have established a good relationship.

LIMITS, SETTING, *See* Boundaries

LINE MANAGERS AS SUPERVISORS, *See* Role conflict, Supervision

LITERAL DESCRIPTION (*See also*: Anger, Experiments, Interpersonal Process Recall)

When clients talk about or 'talk through' painful and difficult experiences, they are naturally drawn into telling their story of what happened in the past tense. They also usually avoid aspects of the experience, search for reasons, explanations or justifications for their emotions or behaviour, and are sometimes circular and repetitive, with a sense of getting nowhere. In these circumstances it can be helpful to encourage clients to intensify and expand their account, through literal description.

The client is invited to describe the past experience in the present tense, to try to relive it in as much detail as possible, recalling colours, sounds, smells, position of objects, people, movements and so on. Clients typically drift back into the past tense, often interpreting or evaluating what had happened and you need to remind them to describe it as if it's happening now, or invite them to say it again in the present tense, e.g. if the client says; 'then I shouted at him' – you might ask the client to say 'I'm shouting at him'.

Literal description is potentially a very powerful intervention and should be used with great care and sensitivity by counsellors who have experienced it themselves. It is best approached by asking clients if they would like to try something – a kind of experiment – to see if it would help them to get in touch with their feelings about what happened and to break through or disengage the story-telling pattern. Evison and Horobin (1983) provide an excellent source for this and similar strategies and techniques for facilitating catharsis and the re-experiencing of emotions (and subsequent insight). Murgatroyd and Woolfe (1982) recommend the possible use of literal description in helping clients in crisis.

LITIGATION, *See,* Insurance (indemnity), Sued (being)

LOVE, ADULT ROMANTIC (*See also*: Framework)

> I do not like to work with patients who are in love.
>
> *Yalom, 1989, p. 15*

Table 5 Some key words for each style of loving (Lee, 1988)

Eros	ideal beauty, immediate physical attraction, delight
Ludus	playful, free of commitment, avoid intensity
Mania	feverish, obsessive, jealous
Storge	friendly, companionable, affectionate
Pragma	practical, realistic, compatible
Storgic eros	friendly intensity
Ludic eros	playful intensity
Storgic ludus	friendly and playful

Within psychology there are four main approaches to understanding love: the social psychological, psychodynamic, cognitive-behavioural and humanistic. In very broad terms, social psychology has studied first attractions and, more recently, questions about maintaining love; the psychodynamic approach recognizes love's passion and drama more, but in a 'dark' way with concepts like 'dovetailing pathology'; cognitive-behavioural theorists focus on learning, rewards and costs, and behaviour, beliefs, needs and expectations, and changing them; and humanistic psychologists generally add a more positive emphasis.

Lee's eclectic approach (e.g. 1988) has some unusual strengths. For example, he distinguishes several kinds or styles of love (see Table 5 for brief definitions) and, in contrast to other typologies of love, sees all the styles as equally 'true'. This can be a severe test of acceptance and empathy (and a stimulating workshop). His theory is flexible as well as pluralistic: most people have a preferred style but each of us can love different partners in different styles, or the same partner in different styles at different times.

Another strength of Lee's theory is that it suggests answers to questions like 'Does real love appear suddenly or gradually'? 'Do I love her more than she loves me'?, and 'Do you really love me'? It can thus encourage greater clarity and tolerance. Lasswell and Lobsenz (1980) discuss applications of Lee's theory in couples' counselling. For reviews of research on love see Sternberg and Barnes (1988) and Shaver and Hazan (1988). Shaver and Hazan's preferred approach is to relate Bowlby's attachment theory to adult romantic love, recognizing the possibility that thinking about and working through unpleasant childhood experiences of relationships helps people change their mental models of relationships.

M

MANIPULATION (*See also*: Drama Triangle, Hidden agenda, Hooked)

Manipulation is a defensive process in which overt or covert pressure is put on another person. In Transactional Analysis terms these are called games and can often be described in terms of the Drama triangle. When somebody is playing a game with you then your interaction with them isn't quite what it seems and you can end up feeling trapped and resentful. For example, if somebody acts as if they are hard done by they may manipulate someone into helping them.

In another case someone may act as though they think they are wonderful, but underneath they are fearful of being rejected. The front is put on as self-protection and with a hope that others will be attracted and not see the frightened person underneath. This type of manipulation often fails as it either attracts the wrong type of person, or else the front is so transparent as to be useless, or cause irritation (Stewart, 1989).

MARKETING (*See also*: Advertising, Nuisance telephone calls)

Marketing is a specialist area, so we will offer only some basic questions, suggest some resources, and indicate some of the difficulties involved in making a living as a counsellor. Perhaps the most basic question of all for many counsellors is whether the idea of 'marketing' clashes with your self-image. The next questions, based on Townsend (1984) are:

- What are you selling? (What is *different* about it or you?)
- Who might want to buy it?
- How do you make contact with them?
- Price?

Which (phone 0800 252100) publish *Starting Your Own Business*, which is a book (240 pp.), and *Working For Yourself*, an action pack on such matters as identifying your 'core business activity', assessing the market and formulating a business plan.

Feltham (1993) gives a sobering analysis of the difficulties for many counsellors of making their living from counselling. He discusses such aspects as the costs (training, supervision, etc.), competition for work, and the problems of juggling a variety of activities. It is a vivid and unglamorous picture.

METAPHORS AND SIMILES (*See also*: Empathy)

Metaphors can be used to describe general approaches to counselling and as a way of communicating empathy. Taking the first of these, which (if any) of the metaphors below are closest to your approach to counselling, and which are definitely not relevant to you?

- as midwife
- as surgeon
- as companion
- as detective
- as archaeologist
- as guide
- as teacher
- as guru
- as consultant

There are two distinct views on the value of metaphors and similes in 'capturing' emotions. One is that – used by client or counsellor – they sometimes express emotions better than more straightforward terms. If a client says 'I feel like a coiled spring' then this may be clearer than 'angry' and 'longing to do something'. Lakoff and Johnson (1980) argue that our conceptual system is fundamentally metaphorical; metaphors structure what we perceive and how we relate to others. The second view is that metaphors are a step towards finding the emotion words that fit. A compromise is that both views are true at various times.

MISSED SESSIONS (*See also*: Clients who don't come back, Contract, Fees, Expectations)

Occasionally a client does not turn up for an appointment, and you may be left wondering why and what to do. To some extent this can be avoided by stating clearly in the contract what notice is expected and what payment is required if a client misses a session. The most straightforward situation is when a client has a regular time, pays in advance and knows that if they miss a session they still pay. Other counsellors work with clients who come at varying times, who pay at the end of each session, or who may not be required to pay at all. The contract in these cases needs to be particularly clear.

Knowing whether to contact a client who has missed a session and how this is to be done can also be covered in the contract. For example some counsellors phone the client after 15 minutes if they have not turned up, to see if they are alright, or have just forgotten. Others write a letter suggesting another date. Occasionally a counsellor states in the contract that a session missed without notice, or without a very good reason, indicates the end of the contract. Generally we advise a short letter as phoning can be intrusive or put the client 'on the spot'.

MISTAKES, *See* Assertiveness, Fear, in the counsellor

MODELS, *See* Theories, Frameworks

MULTICULTURALISM (*See also*: Difficulties in being a client, Psychological type)

Multiculturalism emphasizes a need for counsellors to be much more aware of differences in ethnic origin, gender, social class, disability, age and other factors. For example, d'Ardenne's (1993) view is that counsellors who 'are curious about their clients' cultural backgrounds and are not afraid to acknowledge their ignorance, who can ask about their clients' experiences of alienation within and beyond therapy, are half-way to dealing with the issues' (p. 6). The multicultural approach contrasts with the traditional focus on individuals and on personality, which emphasizes the possibility of change and development for everyone, regardless of multicultural factors, and in which counselling qualities, skills and strategies are seen as generally applicable.

In Bimrose's (1993) framework, the traditional position is termed **Individualistic**. She contrasts it with two others: the **Integrationist**, in which the counsellor adapts to clients more, e.g. by being more active and directive, or acknowledging the central role of oppression in a client's life, and the **Structuralist** which focuses on social conditions as the major causes of individual distress. The framework can help counsellors locate and consider their own positions. An important multicultural issue is how to incorporate it into effective practice, for example the question of whether clients should be 'matched' with counsellors. Chaplin (1993) and Alladin (1993) discuss women counselling women and matching for ethnic origin, respectively. Key sources on multiculturalism are Sue and Sue (1990), and Ivey *et al*. (1993) who see 'the task of the next decade' as a thorough re-examination of counselling from a multicultural perspective.

MUSTS, *See* Thoughts

N

NERVOUS CLIENTS (*See also*: Beginnings, Contract, Difficulties in being a client, Quiet clients, Respect, Silence, Warmth)

There is no sure way of knowing whether a client is nervous or not. Rapid speech, silence, shaking hands, difficulty in speaking may all indicate nervousness but could indicate something else. Being calm, establishing the client's needs, answering questions and empathizing, all usually help nervous clients to feel more relaxed. It may be useful to remember that for many people being a client is difficult.

NON-VERBAL COMMUNICATION, *See* Empathy, Crying, Drawings, Emotions, Exercises, Furniture, Kissing, Paraphrasing, Privacy, Silence, Smoking, Touch

'NO SHOW' CLIENTS, *See* Clients who don't come back, Contract, Defining counselling to clients, Difficulties in being a client, Missed sessions.

NOTE, TAKING (*See also*: Assertiveness, Contract, History taking, Records, Self-awareness)

Although some counsellors take full notes during sessions, most take none at all. Perhaps the question to ask is, 'What do I need these notes for?' If they are to help you build up a picture of your client's concerns and progress, it might be better to write them up immediately after the session. The same goes if you are taking notes to help you make a presentation, or write a case study.

The problem with taking notes during sessions is that they distract your attention away from listening and responding sensitively to your client. It may also have the same distracting effect on your client. Taking notes during sessions may make your client feel more like a 'case' than a person, though you can of course discuss this. However, if your approach to counselling involves asking a lot of questions about family history, early relationships etc. you may need to make a lot of notes, at least early on.

Dalton (1992, pp. 16–18) discusses what happened when she agreed that a client could see her notes, written in a style she describes as 'telegrammatic' and 'unvarnished'. The client was furious with their 'coldness', a reaction which they later agreed was to do with the client's anxieties about being genuinely liked, and about ending counselling. Dalton also discusses her motives for agreeing quickly, and what she is more likely to do in the future: slow down, discuss the reason and explain her style of note-taking.

NUISANCE TELEPHONE CALLS
(*See also*: Answerphone)

Nuisance means different things to different people and there is no definitive categorization of these calls. There does not seem to be any research on calls to counsellors in particular and there is no evidence that counsellors are treated differently from other people. Four kinds of nuisance calls can be suggested:

1. Calls at antisocial times.
2. Frequent calling.
3. Threatening calls.
4. Obscene calls.

The first two categories are potentially less serious. Some counsellors have the times they can be called at home printed on their note paper and report that this reduces the number of calls at other times. Gentle reminders, or information as to what is acceptable by you, may also help in the first two categories. If this fails, the chance for the caller to talk through their need to call may help. When none of these methods work, the calls enter the threatening category.

Threatening and obscene calls have been experienced by the majority of the population, both male and female (Sheffield, 1989; McKinney, 1990), with a large variation in the amount of harassment perceived and received. It is very rare that the calls lead to face-to-face confrontation with the caller. Crisis centres have a high number of obscene calls and also calls from people who make the calls and want to stop.

British Telecom recommend the following:

1. Remain silent and leave the phone off the hook, or unplugged.
2. Hang up.
3. Change telephone numbers.
4. Get the call traced.

If the first two methods don't work, phone 0800 666 777 for recorded advice, and if the calls persist 0800 661 441 for BT's Help Bureau. New systems for tracing calls are much more effective than they used to be, and it is reported that the latest development, to be introduced in 1994, will display a caller's number while the phone rings.

One method that has been found to be very effective is to avoid the usual reaction of fear, anger or upset, which is what the caller hopes for, and to remain very calm and say in a caring voice something like 'Listen to me, you obviously have a problem, I feel very sorry for you and suggest you go for treatment before you get into trouble'.

There is some evidence that a sizeable proportion of the male population have made an obscene call at some time or other (Matek, 1988; Templeman and Sinnett, 1991). Most are young, not dangerous and only mildly disturbed. They can probably be helped by the normal counselling methods. If the counsellor does not feel happy with this it is probably best to refer the client to centres dealing with sexual problems.

NVQs

The National Council for Vocational Qualifications (NCVQ) was set up by the government in 1986 to promote, develop, implement and monitor a comprehensive system of vocational qualifications in the UK. An NVQ framework at levels I–IV, covering qualifications up to and including those based on the higher national standard or its equivalent, in all major employment sectors, has been established. The four levels of competence so far defined are not at professional standard. At the present time there are no units of competence that refer to counselling although various pilot studies have been conducted and draft guidelines are being prepared.

NCVQ
222 Euston Road
London NW1 2BZ

Tel: 071-387 9898

O

OPENNESS, *See* Congruence, Self-disclosure

OFFICE, *See* Furniture

OUTCOME RESEARCH (ON COUNSELLING), *See* Effectiveness

P

PARALLEL PROCESS (*See also*: Challenging, Process, Supervision)

Parallel process is a term for someone's experience in one situation being repeated in another situation. It can be a trap for unwary counsellors or a possible way of understanding your relationship with your client. For example the supervisee might say 'I really don't know how to begin' and the supervisor would work with this difficulty on the assumption that it was also a difficulty for the client. Or the supervisor says 'I feel blamed by you', and then works with this as a feeling that the supervisee may have had during counselling. Some supervisors work most with the 'here and now' on the grounds that it will mirror the 'there and then' of the counselling session itself.

PARAPHRASING (*See also*: Empathy, Emotions, Metaphors, Self-awareness)

When you paraphrase you attempt to restate, in a fresh way, the main part of what someone has said, without adding any of your own ideas, feelings, interpretations, etc. The tone is slightly questioning without being a question, and your aim, in Rice's phrase, is 'to unfold rather than package experience'. The most basic form of paraphrase is 'You feel ... (emotion) because of ...'

A key element in paraphrasing is being in close emotional contact with your client and also clearly separate: neither overidentifying (fusing) nor being coolly distant. Davenport and Pipes (1990), after giving vivid examples of fusing and distance, suggest the analogy of swimming close to a deep, powerful whirlpool: 'the challenge is to be close enough to the emotional energy to understand what the client must be experiencing without getting swept down into the action oneself' (p. 139). Drowning with the client is not helpful, nor is viewing from too far away.

Paraphrasing is an art as well as a skill and therefore can be carried out technically well with poor results, or technically poorly with excellent results (or, of course, both skilfully and artistically, or neither). However, even inane and trite paraphrases (as in computer programs which claim to mimic empathic responses) are sometimes effective in the sense of encouraging clients to explore and clarify.

A key practical question is 'how often do good counsellors paraphrase?' The answer is of course that it depends, but Rogers (e.g. 1987), believed in frequent checks, and Gendlin (1981, p. 19) suggested an *average* of every five or ten sentences. Gendlin's suggestion can be treated too literally! It is a guideline not a rule, and its merit lies in being concrete about the term 'frequent'. Gendlin makes another specific suggestion about frequency: 'Don't let the person say more than you can take in and say back. Interrupt, say back, and let the person go on' (p. 20). If you dislike the word 'interrupt' in this suggestion, you might like to try replacing it with 'contribute'.

A flexible rather than literal approach is also needed in choosing when to use your client's words in a paraphrase. Generally, it is best to use your own words – there is less chance of sounding like a parrot, an echo or a computer program 'counsellor' – but sometimes a word or phrase used by your client is very significant to them and can be included by you (or noted for later).

FURTHER GUIDELINES

The following guidelines are intended to help you check on and refine your own paraphrasing, not to replace the artistic element. They are the equivalent of 'instructions' on practising or reviewing a backhand or a golf swing. The guidelines are organized in four sections: the purposes of paraphrasing; how do you know when you're paraphrasing well?; and less well?; and some subtle aspects of paraphrasing.

Purposes of paraphrasing

- To help clients to listen to themselves and to clarify what they mean, feel and think (usually by putting it into words).
- To help clients to make more sense of what they're troubled by and therefore increase their sense of perspective and control.
- To help you to listen and to communicate in a concrete way what you've understood and what you haven't, and what you are trying to understand.

How do you know when you're paraphrasing well? (Adapted from Gendlin, 1981)

Your client is more likely to:

- say more, and go further 'inside' (may become more focused and intent); or
- sit silently, relieved that they've been understood and accepted (may become more relaxed).

And less well?

Your client is more likely to:

- try to paraphrase what you've said;

- speak more superficially and continue to do so;
- become tense, confused or annoyed. 'I've just said that'; or
- agree in a desultory way.

Some subtle aspects of paraphrasing

- Good paraphrases tend to emphasize those emotions which are clearly experienced or implied by clients and to capture something of clients' experience of their worlds.
- Simple words seem to capture meanings best (perhaps through discouraging intellectualizing).
- Perhaps most important is helping your client find the *right* words – which has been called the Rumpelstiltskin Effect.
- Pausing after clients have recognized or clarified an emotion gives them the space to feel it more, and perhaps also to feel a sense of relief.
- Focusing on the client's frame of reference (which is another way of defining paraphrasing) may also increase clients' sense of responsibility for their reactions.
- If you have understood (or think you've understood) only part of what your client has said, paraphrase that part, and add that you don't understand the rest.
- Pause before you paraphrase or during a paraphrase, and trust yourself to find words which are good enough or better.
- Try including a *little* of your client's emotion or emotions in the way you say the paraphrase.

PATTERNS (*See also*: Brief counselling, Drama Triangle, Emotions, Feelings, Psychological type, Thoughts)

Everybody has a style of behaving which is unique and multi-faceted, and which occurs again and again, thus creating patterns. Some of these patterns are ways of responding to similar situations in habitual and often unconscious ways. Examples are living with or marrying compulsive gamblers or drinkers, clashing with authority figures, and taking a particular stance, like Victim, Persecutor, or Rescuer, or Earth Mother or Psychotherapist. They are dysfunctional when they have a compulsive, 'taking over' quality, and when the person is upset and baffled by them.

Cognitive counselling tries to help clients discover patterns in the way they think. For example some clients have very negative ideas about themselves and/or about others. Helping clients to be aware of these patterns gives them the chance to examine and change them. 'Shoulds', 'oughts' and 'musts' indicate dysfunctional patterns.

Patterns of behaviour suggest early learning. For example, a client who persistently finds it difficult to get on with women may have found his or her mother very difficult, or have had some painful experience relating to her. Psychodynamic approaches, in their traditional form, focus on this kind of pattern; a key issue in counselling, regardless of the truth of the theory, is whether this is the most efficient route to change for all or most clients. Some counsellors normally try simpler, quicker methods first – thought-stopping or assertiveness training for example – and help clients explore early relationships only if necessary.

PEER SUPERVISION (*See also*: Supervision)

Peer supervision is most appropriate for experienced counsellors and is probably best done in a small group. Each person takes a turn at presenting a case or theme for discussion by the group and is given the opportunity to explore particular aspects, as in standard supervision groups. Other group members can be supportive and challenging, and offer alternative ways of thinking about particular issues.

A supervision group should be small enough, and meet often enough, to enable each member to have adequate time for case presentation. A group of four might need to meet every week for about 2 hours. Peer supervision in pairs, using a co-counselling model, can also be very useful.

The advantages of peer supervision groups include the opportunity to hear how others meet and overcome difficulties, to share ideas and information, and to practise being supportive and constructively challenging. The disadvantages include the fact that groups can find themselves short of time to include everyone fully, and that sometimes peer groups become collusive and find it difficult to be challenging. One way to overcome this potential problem is for the group to meet periodically with an 'outside'

facilitator to review its practices and the relationships that have built up among group members (Horton, 1993, p. 24).

The group can also review itself. Hawkins and Shohet (1989, pp. 56–72) suggest six modes of group supervision, focusing respectively on clients; counsellor interventions and strategies; what the counsellor is 'carrying' from a session; the relationship between counsellor and client; parallels between what is happening in the supervisor and in the counselling; and what is stimulated (emotions, values, images) in the members of the group by a particular presentation. Each supervision group is seen as preferring or specializing in one or more of these, and, perhaps inappropriately, neglecting others.

PENCIL AND PAPER EXERCISES (*See also*: Experiments, Challenge, Homework)

Some clients find eye-to-eye/face-to-face contact threatening, especially when talking about some issues, and may find it easier to focus on a form of writing or drawing shared with the counsellor. 'Paper and pencil' exercises can represent or summarize in words, diagrams or pictures what the client is saying, or be a way for the counsellor to explain or challenge. The entry on Life Space Diagrams gives a detailed example of a paper and pencil exercise.

PERSECUTOR, *See* Drama Triangle

PERSONAL COUNSELLING, FOR THE COUNSELLOR

Different approaches to counselling disagree on how necessary it is for counsellors to have their own counselling, especially as part of the training process. For example, most forms of psychodynamic counselling make it a requirement that trainee counsellors have extensive personal counselling, some other approaches advise or strongly recommend, but do not require it, and some regard it as fully optional (see Dryden and Thorne, 1991, for arguments against).

One argument for being a client is that it is the only way to learn what it is like, and is a very important piece of experiential learning. Almost all schools of counselling call upon counsellors to be able to make clear, creative and open relationships with clients, and being counselled is one way of helping counsellors to build such relationships with others. In particular, it helps counsellors become aware of the difficulties clients may sometimes have in making the best use of their counselling time, both for personal growth and in times of crisis.

In training, it is important to find a counsellor who uses a similar model of counselling as in your course.

POST-TRAUMATIC STRESS DISORDER (PTSD) (See also: Abuse, Anger, Anxiety, Crisis counselling, Depression, Diagnosis, Emotions, Stress)

This mental health problem was formally recognized in 1980 by the American Psychiatric Association. The criteria are described in the Diagnostic and Statistical Manual of Mental Disorder (DSM III) (Brammer et al., 1993) as follows:

1. The client must have witnessed or experienced a serious threat to their life, or physical well-being.
2. The client must re-experience the event in some way.
3. The client must persistently avoid stimuli associated with the trauma or experience a numbing of general responsiveness.
4. The client must experience persistent symptoms of increased arousal.
5. Symptoms have lasted at least a month.

Many clients with PTSD also present with anger, anxiety and/or depression, so it is quite likely that the counsellor will be working with a variety of problems. As with any extreme case, it is important to be very clear how you are working and why. Also, a variety of approaches may be helpful, e.g. a peer support group and relaxation exercises. As well as coping with the trauma, a client might also find they can no longer cope with their everyday life as they could before, which adds another burden. If the trauma is very precise, then there is a definite focus to work on, but if it was more prolonged then again there may be a variety of topics to deal with. What is traumatic may not always be obvious (Scott and Stradling, 1992).

Clients who present with various forms of emotional abuse from childhood may also be suffering PTSD.

In the case of sexual or physical abuse the cause may be quite clear, but again there is no clear knowledge of what a child sees as traumatic, particularly at preverbal stages.

POWER (*See also*: Abuse, Assertiveness, Boundaries, Contract, Counselling, 'Empowerment', Endings, Expectations, Furniture, Immediacy, Multiculturalism, Respect, Role conflict, Sexual attraction, Trust)

In most counselling relationships, the counsellor has greater power. Counselling takes place in the counsellor's room, counsellors may be seen as an expert or authority, they probably know more about counselling, clients disclose far more about themselves than counsellors do, and clients are often in a particularly troubled and vulnerable period of their lives.

An imbalance of power makes abuse more likely, and can be an obstacle to the trust and clear communication at the heart of most approaches to counselling. Most counsellors try to reduce the power imbalance and to support clients' responsibility and autonomy. Listening hard to the client is deeply respectful in itself, and so is the process of negotiating a contract. The general principle is to be aware of differences in power, or perceived differences and, as with other differences, to explore it with the client if it's getting in the way of counselling (*See* Immediacy), or as part of your contract with the client, or in re-negotiating the contract.

PREPARATION FOR BEING A CLIENT, *See* Contract, Expectations

PRESENTING CLIENTS, *See* Supervision (presenting clients for)

PRESENTS FROM CLIENTS (*See also*: Assertiveness, Boundaries)

There seems to be nothing inherently wrong with accepting gifts from clients from time to time, particularly when they are tokens of appreciation when counselling is coming to an end, for example. The occasional small gift need not be any cause for concern, and can be enjoyed, but the client who is forever bringing or sending unwanted or expensive gifts can be a problem. Inappropriate gifts are a challenge to boundaries, and your client may be in counselling partly because he or she is confused or unaware about appropriate boundaries, and accepting gifts from such clients can create further problems.

It can be difficult to refuse a gift. Some people can be very hurt or embarrassed by a refusal, so it needs to be done with great sensitivity and, maybe, an awareness that gifts have different significance in different cultures. It may be better to risk the hurt or embarrassment by confronting the issue directly, but how you do this will depend on what approach you take generally to counselling.

In psychodynamic counselling, a client offering a gift may be thought of as exhibiting transference, and you will deal with this in the same way you deal with all forms of transference.

A person-centred counsellor might appreciate the sentiment behind the gift, but want to express his or her own mixed feelings about accepting it. Whichever form of counselling you prefer, it is better to incorporate the 'gift giving' into the counselling directly than to ignore the significance it may have, particularly if it happens often.

PRINCIPLES OF COUNSELLING, *See* Counselling, BAC Basic Principles of

PRIVACY (*See also*: Confidentiality)

Counselling is essentially a private activity, not only in the sense that it is confidential, but also that it needs to take place in a private setting. An effective counselling relationship can only be established in a non-threatening environment in which clients feel safe and secure. Clients need to feel that they can talk about deeply personal and emotional issues without any risk of being disturbed, overheard or seen by others.

In many modern buildings with lightly constructed or poorly insulated partition walls it is easy to hear doors banging and people talking and laughing or answering the telephone. This can be distracting at best, and may well increase a client's anxiety at a time when they already feel vulnerable. They need to feel that nobody will overhear them or suddenly open the door and come into the room. While you may have no or very limited choice where counselling takes

place, it is possible to take some steps to enhance the feeling of privacy:

1. Put a clear PLEASE DON'T DISTURB notice on the door.
2. Ensure that the telephone is turned off or that calls will be automatically redirected.
3. Make sure that clients sit where they cannot see or be seen by people passing outside any window. Net curtains for windows and translucent self-adhesive sheets for glass door panels can help with this. If fire regulations require that the glass panels can be seen through, you can leave a small gap, covering it temporarily when you are counselling.
4. Inform other users of the building, especially of the corridor and adjacent rooms, of your need for absolute privacy and seek their cooperation. If it is impossible to avoid hearing other people outside the room, some counsellors find that it helps clients to tell them that other people are working in the building but that they will not disturb you.
5. Avoid having clients waiting immediately outside the counselling room.

PRIVATE PRACTICE, *See* Marketing

PROCESS (*See also*: Contract, Hidden agendas, Interpersonal Process Recall, Parallel process, Self-awareness)

The term 'process' is widely used in counselling to refer to how something functions rather than the content or task, as in the following:

Personal process is the functioning of an individual. When a counsellor is unable to empathize, it is sometimes referred to as 'the counsellor's process getting in the way'.

Group process also refers to what is happening under the surface. For example a decision has to be made and one member of the group has a need to control, another wants to impress someone else in the group and a third fears being asked to do more work. All these 'hidden agendas' affect the way a group works. Some groups explore the process, while in meetings it is usually the task which is uppermost. However, sometimes the task cannot proceed because the process gets in the way.

PROFESSIONAL DEVELOPMENT

(*See also*: Accreditation, British Association for Counselling, British Psychological Society, Research, Supervision, United Kingdom Council for Psychotherapy)

Professional development includes the following activities: basic and further training; supervision, required throughout a counsellor's working life in the UK and, increasingly, in other countries (Bond, 1993a); membership of bodies like BAC; taking part in workshops, conferences etc; reading books and journals; counselling for oneself; and accreditation, which can be gained through various paths, including the BAC Accreditation Scheme, Association for Student Counselling Scheme, UKCP National Register, BPS Chartered Counselling Psychologist, etc.

More experienced practitioners may develop their work through diversification. Ivey (1987, p. 336) suggest a simplified version of Morrill *et al.*'s cube model for classifying counselling and related activities. The essence of the model can be represented along three dimensions of intervention, each with separate stages, here seen as developmental. The later stages are different, not superior.

1. **Target**: (a) Individual (b) Group (c) Organization
2. **Purpose**: (a) Remedial (b) Preventive (c) Developmental
3. **Approach**: (a) Direct service (b) Consultation and training (c) Research and materials

Most people start counselling by offering a direct service to individual clients. The work tends to be remedial. Counsellors may at some point want to shift the target of their efforts from individuals to couples, families, groups or organizations. They may also be interested in moving from remedial into more psychoeducational work. Social skills, relaxation and assertiveness training are all examples of interventions with a positive, upstream (Egan, 1975) preventive and developmental purpose. The approach to counselling may also develop from working directly with clients to consultation, counsellor training, training of trainers, supervision, research, writing, broadcasting or the production of audio-visual curriculum materials.

PROFESSIONALISM, DEVELOP-MENT OF (*See also*: Accreditation, BAC, BPS, UKCP)

Unlike traditional professions such as medicine and law, there is no statutory body controlling standards of training and practice within counselling. Three principal organizations are involved: the British Association for Counselling (BAC), the UK Council of Psychotherapy (UKCP), and the Counselling Division of the British Psychological Society (BPS). UKCP published its national register in 1993 and the BPS Counselling Division, established in 1994, means that there are now Chartered Counselling Psychologists. BAC, which has a much more catholic representation, has been involved in discussions about the production of a national register of counsellors for some time, and has well established schemes for the accreditation or recognition of counsellors, supervisors and training courses. For many people these schemes spearhead professionalism. A working party has now been set up and a national register of counsellors will probably be introduced in 1994.

The idea of professionalism has not received a unanimous welcome. There are strong feelings of ambivalence, if not unequivocal opposition, especially within BAC. Some people dislike the whole idea of the professional as someone who earns money for doing what others do for pleasure, sense of duty or intrinsic interest (Charles-Edwards *et al.*, 1989). They reject the tendency to mystify and regulate what they see as a fundamental human process that should be available to all. They resent what they see as the setting up of a closed shop or protection racket and strongly deny the assumption that 'non-professionals' necessarily lack skills or experience.

It is hard to see how the advancing wave of professionalism within BPS, UKCP or even within BAC can be stopped, or indeed whether it should be. Perhaps the key issue is whether what is primarily in the interests of the professional counsellor is necessarily to the ultimate benefit of clients.

PSYCHODIAGNOSIS

The best known systems of psychodiagnosis are ICD-10, the World Health Organization's International Classification of Diseases, and DSM-III-R, the American Pychiatric Association's Diagnostic and Statistical Manual of Mental Disorders (Comer, 1992; Brammer *et al.*, 1993). Some counsellors, e.g. Shlien (1989) regard them as a form of evil.

Some of the advantages of psychodiagnosis are as follows:

- It suggests strategies and methods that have been shown to be effective with similar problems.
- It provides a framework for research and for the development of a body of knowledge about various patterns of disorder and ways to treat them.
- Many practitioners find themselves working in mental health agencies where they are required to make diagnostic classification of client problems. This is increasingly linked to health insurance in the USA.

- A classification system enables practitioners and researchers to communicate more easily. It is not necessary to list every one of a client's symptoms in order to discuss the client with a supervisor or colleague. A diagnostic category is sufficient to give a general picture of the kinds of difficulty the client is experiencing, which can then be enhanced by individual detail.

Criticisms of psychodiagnosis include the following:

- Diagnosis often places meaningless and poorly defined labels on clients.
- Labels can become self-fulfilling prophecies when the label is perceived as coming from an 'expert' in human behviour and is interpreted as a statement about the client's general behaviour. Clients can then more easily avoid taking responsibility by 'acting into' the identified symptoms and accepting the patient role.
- Clients diagnosed with particular disorders can be viewed and treated in stereotyped ways by practitioners, friends, relatives and even the clients themselves for a long time after the disorder has disappeared.
- Practitioners can become preoccupied with a client's history and neglect current attitudes and behaviour, losing sight of the client's individual and unique experience.
- Since diagnosis has been associated historically with pathology, there is a danger that counsellors will be preoccupied with pathology and under-estimate or exclude clients' strengths and resources.
- There is a risk of gender role-socialization influencing diagnosis. For example, women socialized into being emotionally expressive and putting the needs of others ahead of their own may be vulnerable to being diagnosed in particular ways (e.g. histrionic or dependent). Similarly, men socialized into being more distant rather than engaging with others may be seen as paranoid or antisocial. In this way diagnosis may reflect the potential for seeing as pathological those aspects of behaviour that are normative for women/men who have been well socialized.
- Sociocultural influences result in people from particular cultural/ethnic groups being vulnerable to inaccurate diagnosis.
- An emphasis on diagnosis can encourage client dependence on experts.
- Practitioners need to be adequately trained to use the various systems which still have relatively low reliability and validity.
- The use of psychodiagnosis can appear on the surface as eminently scientific and objective, thus heightening the mystique of professionalism and investing practitioners with authority.

PSYCHOLOGICAL TYPE (*See also*: 'Good counsellors', Theory)

Psychological type is a theory of personality developed by Myers (1980) from some of Jung's ideas. She suggests 16 'kinds of people', describing all 16 primarily in terms of strengths and potential strengths. The evidence for the theory is promising, especially its relationship with the 'Big Five' factor theory of personality currently dominating personality research (Bayne, 1994).

Type is relevant to counselling in several ways:

1. As an approach to elements of the counsellor's self-awareness.
2. As a way of understanding and accepting four major ways in which clients' personalities vary.
3. As a type theory, i.e. going beyond the four major ways to suggest how each person's personality is organized.
4. As an approach to personality development and self-esteem, i.e. different types have different patterns of development and find self-esteem in very different experiences.

The psychological type of your client is relevant to many aspects of counselling, e.g. when:

- negotiating a contract (e.g. the types tend to have different expectations of counselling);
- being empathic and accepting;

Table 6 Clients' preferences and behaviour in counselling

Clients who prefer:	tend to:
Extraversion	• want a more active counsellor • be less comfortable with reflection
Introversion	• be more at ease with silence • be less comfortable with action
Sensing	• be concrete and detailed • go step by step • not see many options
Intuition	• give broad pictures • jump around from topic to topic • see unrealistic options • see lots of options
Thinking	• avoid feelings and values in early sessions • need rationales • be critical
Feeling	• focus on values and networks of values • need to care • be 'good clients'
Judging	• fear losing control • find change stressful • need structure
Perceiving	• avoid decisions • need flexibility

- challenging (if appropriate); and/ or
- helping clients set goals or take action (if appropriate).

Type theory suggests that people prefer and are more comfortable with some ways of experiencing and behaving than others. Table 6 lists these (called preferences) and the implications for clients' behaviour, in counselling and generally. It does not take type development, or other factors affecting behaviour, into account.

The implications for counselling of the tendencies listed in Table 6 follow fairly directly, e.g. if you're an Introvert counsellor with an Extrovert client, to consider being more active or at least discussing this with your client. The general principle here is the standard one of discussing relevant aspects of your relationship, for example, using the skill of immediacy, to say 'I wonder if you're finding it difficult when I don't say anything'. A second general principle is to counsel mainly in your own way but to adapt to clients a little. An alternative view here is that the counsellor should first 'talk the language' of each client's type – starting where the client is – then gradually 'pull back somewhat to their own style' (Provost, 1984, p. 129), but this may ask most counsellors to be too versatile.

Myers (1980) is a key source on type. Bayne (1993) and Provost (1984) focus on type and counselling. Bayne outlines the theory and includes a table for counsellors similar to the one above; Provost's book is mainly a set of brief case studies, on counselling someone of each of the types.

Q

QUESTIONS (*See also*: Challenge, Empathy, Paraphrasing, Summaries)

Questions can be the most ensnaring of all skills. In searching for an answer or way to help the client, it can be tempting to take the role of a traditional doctor and ask a series of diagnostic questions. This can easily set up a pattern of question and answer leading to other questions and more answers, with the questioner controlling the direction of the exploration and holding on to the power in the relationship. This type of interaction does little to establish a warm and positive climate in which clients are encouraged to take responsibility. Yet sometimes questions are useful in counselling. As Benjamin, writing about what he refers to as his 'battle' with the use of the question, says: 'I meant to dethrone it but not drive it out' (1969, p. 90).

Egan (1990) suggests that the next intervention following a question should never be another question. It is helpful to reflect on whether the question you are about to ask will inhibit or further the flow of the session and in what way the answer to the question will help you to help the client or whether it will merely satisfy your curiosity. Very brief questions, e.g. 'And you?' 'And?' 'But?' (each of which is a challenge) can occasionally be useful, but generally we suggest asking very few questions. For detailed discussion of types of question, etc. see Dillon (1990) and Brammer *et al*. (1993).

QUESTIONS (PERSONAL), ASKED BY CLIENTS (*See also*: Assertiveness, Boundaries, Self-disclosure, Trust)

Clients sometimes ask questions like 'Are *you* married'?, 'Do you like football?', or 'Have you been depressed?' How you answer depends to some extent on your model of counselling and the particular circumstances (including how much you're taken by surprise!). One option is a brief, direct answer and an immediate return of focus to the client. For example, 'Yes, I am. Does it make a difference to you?', or 'No, I haven't. Would you feel more understood or optimistic if I had?' If you have a sense of what lies behind the question, you can reflect that to the client, who may not want a literal answer but is saying something about him or herself or their attitude towards you. Another possibility, though one that runs the risk of sounding like a stereotype psychoanalyst, is to say something like 'I find that an interesting question for you to ask. Can you say what lies behind it?' or – more bluntly – 'What's the statement behind that question'?

A general factor is the client's emotional state: whether she or he is feeling vulnerable and insecure, or curious and challenging. For example:

1. **Can I have your home phone number?** If your client is in a state of acute crisis, then it may seem to you more reasonable to agree. Saying no, of course, is being clear about a boundary and encouraging independence.
2. **What training did you do?** A brief, direct reply seems appropriate, preferably said positively and with confidence. The underlying questions, as with criticisms of you as too young, etc., may be: 'What are you like?' and 'Can I trust you?', so you might also say, for example, 'No, I'm not HIV positive but I've spent some time learning about it, and I'd like to try to understand what it's like for you'.

QUIET CLIENTS (*See also*: Contracts, Contraindications, Difficult clients, Reluctant clients, Silence, Trust)

There are many reasons for clients being quiet: they may be reluctant, resistant or stuck, they may not know what is expected of them, they may be a quiet person, or they may be reflecting. The most important point seems to be whether the silence is beneficial to the client. They may need time to adapt to you, or to trust you. They may need time to think, or to summon up the courage to take responsibility for themselves. It is for you to establish whether they have a problem with silence and if so why. It is also for you to establish that clients know what is expected in the session and if they really want to be there at all.

R

RAPPORT (*See also*: Congruence, Core conditions, Contract, Psychological type, Readiness to change, Referral, Working alliance)

Rapport, according to Rowan (1983) means, 'being connected to the other person, relating well to the other person, being on the same wavelength, being able to communicate well, and so on'. Establishing rapport with a new client is not always easy but it is a very important part of the initial stages of counselling. Rowan (1983) takes advice from Bandler and Grinder who are well known in the field of Neuro Linguistic Programming (NLP). They advocate taking your cue from your client by copying the way they speak, use visual images, and so on. This is too mechanical and contrived for some tastes, and there is a danger that if it is done inexpertly it will be experienced by clients as a form of mimicry, which can be very uncomfortable.

This form of 'mirroring' as it is known, could also conflict with being congruent and natural, but obviously it helps to establish rapport if your way of speaking and the language you use is not completely at odds with your client. In the initial stages of counselling you will be concentrating on listening to and understanding your client, and this includes being aware of your client's way of expression and language. It is possible to maintain your own natural and spontaneous 'way of being' while remaining sensitive to your client's manner and mood. The important thing is to take your time, and 'tune in' to your client gradually without trying to force yourself to establish instant rapport before either of you are ready.

RAPPROCHEMENT, *See* Common factors, Integration and eclecticism

READINESS TO CHANGE (*See also*: Assessment, Contraindications, Expectations, Furniture, Working alliance)

Some people take to counselling much

more easily than others. Counselling cannot begin until people recognize their need to change and until they are at least some way towards committing themselves to change.

Prochaska and DiClemente (1984) suggest the following model for assessing how ready a person is to change. There are four stages:

1. **Precontemplation**: In this stage people see little or no point in counselling, at least for themselves. They are 'reluctant clients' who have usually been persuaded by friends or relations to try counselling. They are clearly sceptical and doubt its value even though they may admit that they would like things or people around them to be different. Reluctant clients tend to drop out quickly.

2. **Contemplation**: In this stage people recognize that they have a problem and are thinking seriously about what they might do about it. They are not fully committed to the idea of counselling, but tend to be open to exploration and willing to talk about themselves and their problem.

3. **Action**: In this stage, people have tried different ways of coping with their problems. They have some understanding of themselves and the nature of the problem. Often they have clear ideas about what they want to do. People in this stage are genuinely prepared to commit themselves to counselling, but may be impatient to move forward rather than explore and clarify.

4. **Maintenance**: In this stage, people tend to have already made significant changes in their lives. They may have had previously positive experiences of counselling and be fully committed to its value. They seek counselling at this stage to reinforce earlier gains and develop new strategies and coping skills to prevent the recurrence of problems and to find more positive ways of living.

Dryden and Feltham (1992) argue that counsellors need to be able to recognize a client's probable stage of readiness to change. They warn that difficulties will arise if you attempt to apply a single therapeutic approach to all clients, irrespective of the stage they are in. Several factors appear to contribute to higher levels of client readiness. Brammer et al., (1993), for example suggest positive and realistic expectations of counselling and/or the counsellor; intellectual curiosity; willingness to self disclose; flexible attitudes and defence systems; openness to new perspectives; high level of commitment to counselling; comfortable physical surroundings; and a sense of the counsellor as aware of and sympathetic to any cultural and ethnic differences. A further factor is that most counsellors like working with young, imaginative, sensitive, curious, intelligent and anxious clients (Brammer et al., 1993).

RECOGNITION, BY BAC, OF COUN-SELLOR EDUCATION/TRAINING COURSES IN THE UK (*See also*: Accreditation, British Association for Counselling, Complaints, Counselling, Professionalism, Validation (of counsellor education/training courses in the UK))

Over the past decade there has been an enormous expansion in the provision of counsellor education and training in the UK. It has become very difficult for people who want to train as counsellors, or for counsellors who want to do further training, to know which are likely to be good courses. Similarly, organizations wanting to employ counsellors are often ill-informed about the level and quality of training which they should be seeking in applicants. To help potential students, employers and clients to identify high standards of training, the British Association for Counselling (BAC) established the Courses Recognition Scheme. This validates in-depth training courses. 'In depth' is defined as one year full-time or two/three years part-time, to satisfy the minimum 450 hours staff–student contact time.

The Courses Recognition Scheme was launched in 1988, after 4 years of consultation and research. Its aim is to recognize training programmes of very different orientations and traditions. The criteria and guidelines published in the booklet *The Recognition of Counsellor Training Courses* (BAC, 1990) seek to preserve and enhance the independence of approaches while at the same time ensuring that adequate attention is paid to what are regarded as the core elements of training. Thus a course, whatever its rationale, must be able to satisfy the minimum criteria for each of eight core elements: Admission, Self-development, Client work, Supervision, Skills training, Theory, Professional development and Assessment. The minimum standards include providing an in-depth training in a particular core theoretical model of counselling, an appropriate balance among the academic, personal development and skill components, consistent with that model, and students each completing not less than 100 hours of client work during the course, with regular clinical supervision. The scheme also emphasizes that courses should be staffed by appropriately qualified and experienced practitioners, the majority of whom should be BAC-accredited counsellors or at least eligible for accreditation.

A further implication of being a BAC-recognized course is that the course is an organizational member of the BAC and thereby subject to its complaints and appeals procedures. This has an important function for consumer protection, as a course can lose its recognized status for any breaches of the Codes of Ethics and Practice. The Courses Recognition Scheme, like other forms of validation or accreditation, is concerned with design, development and adequate resources, but (unlike them) is primarily concerned with operation and delivery. It is especially interested in the way in which the course gathers feedback and evaluation from staff, students and external examiners and how this is used to modify and improve the programme.

The process of applying for recognition is in several stages. The intention is to identify as early on as possible those courses that are not suitable for the scheme. This saves wasting time and money working through the entire procedure only to then find the scheme is inappropriate for the particular course. Courses are strongly advised to start by arranging a consultation in order to clarify their eligibility for the scheme, before preparing the substantial submission document. At the application stage each member of the BAC panel examines the document, often requesting further information or clarification from the course. When they are satisfied that the course meets the criteria on paper, they move into the visit stage and see the course in action. Panel members observe teaching sessions and supervision groups, talk to past and present students, examine written work, view the facilities and talk to members of staff. The Panel then decide whether to award Recognized status or if certain conditions have first to be met. The course receives a full report. Recognized courses are required to consult with another recognized course throughout the 5-year partnership stage, after which they apply for re-recognition.

The Courses Recognition Scheme is essentially a peer evaluation scheme. Panels are drawn from core staff representatives of recognized courses who together form the BAC Courses Recognition Group (CRG) which is responsible for the management and operation of the scheme. In this way the scheme receives continual feedback and is subject to modification and refinement – learning from the experience of those who have worked through the process. The CRG is accountable to the Accreditation and Recognition Subcommittee and ultimately to the membership through the Management Committee of BAC.

In 1993 there were 16 recognized courses, but the very large number of enquiries, requests for advice and consultations and the sales of the relevant BAC booklet, now in its second edition, are indicative of the impact of the scheme on counsellor education and training in the UK.

RECORD KEEPING (*See also*: Confidentiality, Notes, Sued (being), Suicide)

BAC do not at present (September, 1993) require or recommend that counsellors keep records, though Bond (1993a) thinks they will. The arguments for keeping records include:

1. Writing them helps to organize your thoughts and feelings (though this is an argument for writing rather than for keeping what you write);
2. they are an aid to memory and planning;
3. they provide evidence of any change;
4. they provide evidence of care and professional responsibility.

The arguments against include:

1. avoiding problems of confidentiality and security;

2. they take time;
3. clients may wish to see them (Bond, 1993a, pp. 165–67).

What may matter more than the arguments listed above is your model of counselling. How much do you need to remember, and how much would your clients like you to remember? If you do keep records, Bond's discussions of issues like who has access to them, their use in court, their content and format, where and how they are kept, and how long to keep them, are likely to be useful (1993a, pp. 167–79).

REFERRAL (*See also*: Boundaries, Contraindications, Endings, First impressions, Values)

You will not be the best available counsellor for every client or every type of problem, and this may become apparent at any stage of counselling a particular client. However, you may have mixed feelings about referral. You may feel inadequate or ambivalent, experiencing both a sense of failure and relief about referring your client. The following are some of the circumstances in which it is ethically responsible and appropriate for you to make a referral:

1. The client wishes to be referred.
2. The client needs longer-term work, an open-ended contract, or more frequent sessions than you have available, or, if you work for an agency, are possible within the constraints of the agency's policy.
3. You feel overwhelmed, do not understand or have insufficient training or experience to deal with the presenting problem.
4. The presenting problem is one for which other more appropriate or specialist agencies exist. Similarly, at a later or action-planning stage of counselling it becomes apparent that the client needs more specialist advice, information, longer-term counselling, or practical help.
5. The client persistently fails to respond to your counselling and may be helped more effectively by someone else.
6. The client needs medical attention.
7. The client shows signs of severe mental illness and is not able to continue without intensive care and support.
8. There is in your view a real risk of harm to the client or others.
9. You or the client are leaving the area to live somewhere else.
10. You experience a very strong negative reaction to a client or there is a clash of personalities.
11. You discover that you and your client share a close relationship.

You and your clients can experience a whole range of emotions about referral. While it can bring a real sense of relief and hope, referral can also be disruptive and disappointing. Clients can feel hurt, rejected and reluctant to start again with someone else, or that counselling is not for them anyway. Those who have been passed on from one mental health agency to another may come to believe that their problem is too big for any counsellor and that they are beyond help. Other clients in similar situations feel powerless and become very angry. Referrals in the early stage of the relationship are likely to be less emotionally fraught for both client and counsellor.

Whenever the possibility of referral arises, it is always appropriate that a decision about it is made with the client, although the initial suggestion may come from you. The process can be brief or take a number of weeks or longer, and you may wish to serve as a 'bridge' and provide short-term supportive counselling. Facilitating any referral involves a number of tasks to ensure as far as possible that clients feel generally positive about it:

- Checking that the agency or individual will be able to accept the referral.
- Helping clients explore and perhaps resolve any emotional blocks towards the agency or referral.
- Working towards bringing clients' perceptions of the problem close enough to that of the referral agency for the referral to 'take'.
- Explaining the nature of the help that might be offered and perhaps encouraging the client to consider accepting the help.
- Helping clients if necessary to make their own approach or application.

- Reviewing what has been achieved with clients and exploring what still needs to be achieved and how the referral agency may contribute to this.
- Anticipating and exploring ways of coping with possible differences and potential difficulties in starting work with someone else.
- Letting clients know that referral doesn't end your care and concern.

In order to increase the number of options and establish an efficient referral system you need to develop your own personal contacts and resources file, with people in a variety of occupations – lawyers, osteopaths, psychiatrists, but particularly counsellors and psychotherapists with different strengths and specialisms from your own. Lazarus gives some subtle examples of the matching involved, e.g. referring to somebody who 'has a way with certain words', and also suggests a form of words for referring a client when you are 'stuck': 'I think we need a second opinion here, I am missing something; I have a high regard for my colleague so and so, and would recommend that you see him or her' (Dryden, 1991, p. 32). The words of course reveal something of Lazarus' model of counselling.

In addition to the nature of the help offered by an agency or individual, it is useful for your resources file to contain adequate information on each agency, e.g.

- name of the contact person, telephone number and address;

- whether they offer a 24-hour service, drop-in or appointment system;
- scale of fees charged, if any, or if financial assistance is available;
- likely waiting time;
- how the referral can be made and by whom;
- whether they offer a telephone service;
- whether they send information or publications;
- theoretical orientation of counsellors;
- training and supervision of counsellors;
- code of ethics to which counsellors subscribe;
- whether the agency offers individual and/or group counselling.

REFLECTION OF FEELINGS (*See also*: Core conditions, Emotions, Empathy, Feelings, Paraphrasing)

Most counsellors would associate 'reflection of feelings' with Carl Rogers and client-centred counselling, but it is now widely used, and part of the range of methods or techniques within almost all approaches to counselling. Reflection of feelings is a way of communicating empathic understanding, but Rogers became increasingly concerned that it was being misrepresented as a simple and rather mechanical technique. For him empathy was not a matter of 'reflection' in the way a mirror reflects, which he thought was a rather passive process. Rather, he was trying to establish the extent to which his understanding of his clients was accurate, and his responses contained the unspoken question, 'Is this the way the world feels to you at the moment?' Rogers' preferred terms, later in his life, were 'testing understanding', or 'checking perceptions', where he tried to emphasize the active process involved in both gaining deeper empathic understanding and communicating it.

REGULARITY OF SESSIONS (*See also*: Boundaries, Contract, Power, Working alliance)

Some clients appreciate being offered the same day of the week, and the same time of day for their counselling sessions. This has at least three possible advantages. First, you may be seen as consistent and reliable, which will help you establish trust with your client. Second, your client may be able to arrange for time away from work or home more easily, especially if childcare arrangements are necessary. Third, they may also help to maintain the working alliance as purposeful and concentrated. On the other hand, some clients and counsellors need flexibility, and short 'bursts' of counselling with gaps may help some clients change more effectively.

RELATIONSHIP, BETWEEN COUNSELLOR AND CLIENT, *See* Common factors, Core qualities, Counselling, Empathy, Rapport, Trust

RELUCTANT CLIENTS (*See also*: Avoidance, Denial, Difficult clients, Empathy, Expectations, Information, Quiet clients, Referral)

Clients can see counselling as a luxury or a necessity, but want, at least in part, to be there. They may also see it as an admission of failure, or an indication that they are losing their sanity, and therefore be wary of attending. Moreover, some clients are coerced into coming by others, e.g. family, or an institution. Children nearly always attend at the insistence of others. The reasons for a client's reluctance need to be clarified – they may be anything from lack of information to a deep-seated fear – and clients need to be aware that their needs come first. Queries need to be answered; confidentiality assured. Some clients like to know about the Code of Ethics. Good use of listening skills, empathy and information giving are all central to responding well to reluctant clients.

RESCUING, *See* Drama Triangle

RESEARCH

Research is helpful in two ways: first, its existence makes critical thinking and concern for evidence more likely, second, there are some useful studies and there will be more. The following study is described as an example of a potentially useful piece of research. Clarke and Greenberg (1986) compared the effectiveness of two kinds of intervention intended to help clients with decisions: One (problem-solving) intended to help clients change their way of thinking, the other (Gestalt two-chair method) focused more on emotions. The study was thus relevant to theoretical issues too, particularly controversy about the relative importance of thoughts and emotions.

In the study, four counsellors trained in two-chair method and four trained in problem-solving each saw four clients, all of whom were volunteers facing a 'difficult, personal decision'. There was also a waiting list group. There were lots of good methodological points in the research design, e.g. the eight counsellors were equally experienced in and positive about their own approach, and the sessions themselves were taped so that they could be rated for actual use of the two approaches. You may at this point like to predict the result.

The study showed that both methods reduced indecision more effectively than being on the waiting list, and that the two-chair method was the most effective. The authors then discussed the strengths and limitations of their study, but perhaps the main point is that Clarke and Greenberg were doing what most counsellors do anyway – comparing different methods to help them decide which is 'best' – but doing it in a more systematic and explicit way.

Perhaps the best approach to finding useful research is to skim journals, finding the articles that interest you most, and considering (i) their value to you in your counselling, and (ii) whether they raise questions that you would like to do research on, or a method that you would like to try out.

A much wider range of methods (qualitative and quantitative) is gradually becoming accepted (Heppner et al., 1992; Orford, 1992, Chapter 6).

Lewis (1993) argues that the term 'research' is a very loaded one, and best interpreted as 'finding out' rather than anything mysterious (though some journals seem to do their best to be unreadable). Lewis also discusses ways of getting closer to formal research – he takes the conventional journal paper apart – how to evaluate it, and how to use it. A special issue of *American Psychologist* (1986, 41(2) reviewed the general issue of psychotherapy research and practice. Barkham (1993b) discusses some examples of research findings useful to counsellors but suggests that 'it is likely that practitioners will continue to be disappointed' (p. 141), though his own reviews (e.g. 1990, 1993a) are often clear and practical. For the formal researcher (even though it often exemplifies why practitioners tend to ignore research), Bergin and Garfield's Handbook (1994) is essential.

RESISTANCE, *See* Avoidance

RESPECT (*See also*: Counselling, Core conditions, Warmth)

Respect, also referred to as acceptance and warmth, is considered by most approaches to counselling to be a highly desirable characteristic of the counsellor. Its essential quality is that it is as non-judgemental and unevaluative as possible. It is not the same as 'liking' or 'feeling affection', and

it is not an instruction to counsellors about how they should feel for their clients. Rather, it is a lack of judgement of a client's present way of being, and an acceptance that positive change is possible, even for clients whose behaviour may at present be very destructive towards self or others (Rogers, 1961; Mearns and Thorne, 1988; Merry and Lusty, 1993).

RESTIMULATION, *See* First impressions, Patterns, Transference

ROLE CONFLICT (*See also*: Boundaries, Brief counselling, Confidentiality, Counselling, Effectiveness, Power, Self-awareness, Stress)

For some people, counselling is part of a wider professional role. For example, some teachers and nurses offer counselling as one of several ways in which they respond to the needs of others. It is not easy to maintain boundaries between different helping roles with the same person, but many helping professionals are able to achieve this. They seem able to build on their existing relationships, established through their other roles, and offer valuable counselling. Another factor is that some people won't go to a counsellor they don't know, but feel comfortable being counselled by a nurse or teacher they have already learnt to trust and respect.

Providing that the distinction between counselling and any other form of helping is explicit, there doesn't seem to be any ethical objection to someone offering counselling to the same person with whom they have, or have had, another role relationship. However, role conflict (as the term suggests) does tend to create some difficulties and five of these are discussed briefly below:

1. **Internal conflict**. It can be very difficult and professionally demanding for the same person in one role to be the expert – with in-depth knowledge of a particular field, efficient and skilled in performing tasks *for* others – and then to switch roles, and provide a helping relationship in which the responsibility is on the client to work through and come to terms with painful and emotional aspects of their life.

2. **Expectations**. The client is also asked to adapt. In the one role they can expect the nurse or teacher to know the answer, to be able to make things better, but, in the client role they find they can no longer expect things to be made to happen for them in the same way. You may then have to accept their hostility or disappointment, and in turn can doubt your ability as a counsellor. Clearly this is a familiar difficulty any counsellor might face at some time or other with any client, not just those who are having to switch roles with the same person. Nevertheless, role conflict can intensify it, and it can be very hard and often discouraging to deliberately resist a client's expectation of us to be someone who has the answer.

3. **Power**. Perhaps anyone who sets themselves up to help others in any professional helping role, not just as a counsellor, will automatically become 'superior'. Neutrality in any helping role, including counselling, is probably a myth. The very fact that counsellors place themselves in the position of offering help puts them in a potentially powerful position over the one who temporarily accepts that help. This can feel good and be very seductive. What is important is that counsellors recognize this aspect of the counsellor–client relationship so that it can be appropriately controlled and used (Egan, 1990) or, alternatively, put aside as far as possible (Rogers, 1987).

4. **Individual needs**. Relatively little is known about why people become counsellors. It may reflect a special need to help others and to be needed. This source of satisfaction from counselling is ethical unless clients are exploited. A safeguard is to ensure that you meet most of your needs sufficiently in your own personal life. Counsellors need to monitor what is going on for them and to be aware of the ways in which they might misuse their relationships with clients.

5. **Pressure of work**. Professional helpers tend to be very busy. Within the current ethos of quality control and accountability, there is a pressure to get things done as quickly and efficiently as possible so that more can be done for more people. Employers expect results.

The difficulty for counselling is that it takes time – sometimes weeks or months to establish an effective working relationship with clients and allow them time to explore and work through their problem and find what is the best way of coping effectively. It is very tempting to tell clients what to do, what to think and feel in order (on the surface) to manage or resolve their problems quickly. Counselling doesn't work like this, but it can be difficult (especially for someone who offers counselling as one of several ways of helping) to put these pressures aside.

ROOM, *See* Furniture

S

SAFETY, *See* Personal security, Violence and its prevention

SELF-AWARENESS (*See also*: Assertiveness, Drama Triangle, Emotions, Feelings, Immediacy, Interpersonal Process Recall, Journal, Metaphors, Patterns, Psychological type, Thoughts, Values)

All the 'core qualities' and many of the skills of counselling require at least a reasonable degree of self-awareness, in the sense of awareness of your own thoughts, emotions, sensations, intuitions, intentions, fantasies, images. If we become clearer about ourselves in this 'inside' sense, we can:

- be clearer with other people;
- detect signs of stress earlier;
- have more information on which to base decisions;
- be more ourselves;
- maintain a balance between over-involvement (with consequent stress) and too great a detachment.

Three senses of the term self-awareness are distinguished in Figure 2. First, **inner** self-awareness, as defined above. Second, **self-knowledge**, which refers to relatively stable aspects of inner self-awareness, such as talents,

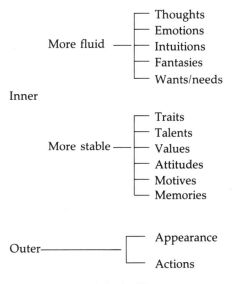

Figure 2: A model of self-awareness.

values, interests and personality traits. Third, **outer** self-awareness, which refers to awareness of your own behaviour, and of how it tends to be interpreted by others.

Counsellor education and training focuses on all three senses of self-awareness, because all three have an impact on counselling. Inner self-awareness provides personal experience, especially emotions, intuitions and insights. Self-knowledge affects your judgements of others, and their judgements of you. Outer self-awareness may need to be referred to, e.g. 'I frowned then because . . .' or 'I was being flippant. There is a serious point there too . . . '.

The idea that we can become more aware of our emotions through counselling, or other ways of focusing attention inwards, applies to the other elements too, and to patterns of emotional responses to people and events, e.g. the Drama triangle. There are of course numerous approaches to increasing self-awareness (e.g. Bond, 1986; Dickson, 1987; Merry and Lusty, 1993). A central quality of self-awareness is that it changes, partly because we change; partly because it is not something that can be finally achieved.

SELF-DISCLOSURE, BY COUN-SELLORS (*See also*: Answerphone, Challenge, Congruence, Crisis (for the counsellor), Furniture, Immediacy, Questions (personal), Self-awareness, Trust)

Three senses of self-disclosure can be distinguished: historical revelation (e.g. I've been jealous too), expressing 'here and now' reactions (e.g. I'm feeling stuck), and non-verbal (e.g. furniture, facial expression). The first should probably be rare in counselling, though occasionally very helpful, the second is a normal part of some approaches to counselling, and the third inevitable.

Self-disclosure in the historical revelation sense can be a useful model for clients who find talking about themselves difficult. The risks, however, are substantial. In particular, the client may be baffled and perhaps try to help the counsellor. It follows that your purpose in self-disclosing should be clear to both counsellor and client, and that you should be direct, brief and relevant.

SEXUAL ATTRACTION (*See also*: Assertiveness, Boundaries, Codes of ethics, Immediacy, Self-awareness, Transference)

OF CLIENTS FOR COUNSELLORS

Clients often enter counselling at times when they feel most vulnerable, after the breakdown of an important relationship, for example, and in particular need of understanding and warmth. It is not surprising, therefore, that clients sometimes become sexually attracted to their counsellors, especially when they feel accepted and valued by you.

Occasionally, clients make sexual suggestions or advances to their counsellors. Some forms of counselling, particularly psychodynamic counselling view this as a form of 'transference' (having feelings for the counsellor which originate in, and belong to, past relationships). Whatever the theoretical explanation, it is most important to hear and acknowledge such feelings, but never directly to act on them. It is best to respond with a gentle, but firm 'No', and to do this in such a way that your client will not feel rejected as a person.

A brief explanation in terms of ethics and boundaries is also likely to be appropriate; then of course it is a matter of listening to your client's reaction and (again, if appropriate and consistent with your approach to counselling) some disclosure of your own reactions. To give a rather clinical perspective, this is modelling the difference between expressing feelings on the one hand and acting on those feelings on the other.

OF COUNSELLORS FOR CLIENTS
(*See also*: Abuse, Boundaries, Immediacy, Power)

The counselling relationship can be very special and close. Counsellors may feel great warmth and love for clients, and sometimes feelings of sexual attraction. This is not a matter of shame or even regret. However, it is important both to acknowledge these feelings and not to act on them directly. Acknowledging them may mean talking about them with someone you trust, perhaps a supervisor or supervision group, though this may feel risky. Some approaches to counselling suggest sharing your feelings with your client. This may, in some

circumstances, be sound advice, but we suggest caution and (perhaps in supervision) a role-play first.

Becoming sexually involved with a client is always unethical, though defining 'sexual' can be a problem (Russell, 1993). It is most important to protect the integrity of the counselling relationship, to be sensitive to and caring of the needs and feelings of your client, to protect and value the professional nature of the counselling activity, and to be true to your own professional, ethical and moral standards. Bond argues that the priority of your concerns should be the client, professional issues and the counsellor, in that order (1993d, p. 111).

The ethics of sexual involvement with an ex-client are more arguable. Russell (1993) argues, on the basis of models of loss and grief, for a 6-month period before ex-clients (not counsellors) make contact socially, and current opinion seems to be moving towards a 'cooling off' period, depending on such factors as the length and nature of the counselling relationship (Bond, 1993a, 1993b, 1993d). The idea of imposing an absolute ban does not do justice to the possibility of love between counsellor and ex-client, rather than an exploitative relationship or a misuse of power. Bond's final point gets to the heart of the debate within BAC: 'The regulations will need to be appropriately protective of clients' interests but without infantilizing them or ignoring their right to act autonomously once the counsellor–client relationship is truly ended' (1993b, p. 107). But, as he earlier points out, *some* counsellors believe that some or all counselling relationships are never ended.

A 1993 addition to the BAC Code of Ethics and Practice for Counsellors states in part that counsellors 'remain accountable for relationships with former clients. ... Any changes in relationship must be discussed in counselling supervision, but also that counsellors who belong to organisations which prohibit sex with all former clients are bound by that commitment.'

SHORT-TERM COUNSELLING, *See* Brief counselling

SHOULDS, *See* Thoughts

SILENCE (*See also*: Empathy, Immediacy, Paraphrasing, Questions)

Silence – giving your client some 'space' – can be very caring and effective, depending on the kind of silence. Some silences are 'working' ones: your client is trying to clarify or disentangle something. Others are natural breaks; there is nothing more to say about something, at least for the moment. These silences can be very peaceful.

Other silences are lost, rejecting or hostile; your client has had enough or is stuck. The best option here is probably to try to be (gently) empathic, e.g. 'You seem very fed up with this?' or 'You're finding it difficult to talk about?' If you can't tell from the context or the client's expression what is going on, you can say something like:

'We've been quiet for some time. I'm not sure what's happening. ...'

SMOKING (*See also*: Boundaries, Stress)

If you don't smoke and you don't like smoking, you have a right to establish this as part of the 'contract' with your clients. Provided your clients know beforehand that they cannot smoke, they will decide whether to continue with you or not. Most people who smoke will be able to accept a 'no smoking' agreement.

In the same way, if you smoke and would like to smoke during the sessions (or in the room between sessions), it is a good idea to discuss this with your clients before the counselling starts. Some people are allergic to tobacco smoke, or become very physically distressed by it, others don't mind at all. Some even enjoy tobacco smoke, even when they don't smoke themselves. If you are not a heavy smoker, you will probably be able to smoke with some clients and not others, but remember that stale tobacco smoke is disliked by many people, even when there is no smoking going on at the time. It tends to linger on clothes and curtains.

Smoking is an addiction, and some people can find it intensely uncomfortable, even painful, to go without it for very long, especially if they become emotional or distressd. The best overall principles therefore seem to be being clear about your attitude to smoking with your clients, and doing your best to respect both your needs and your clients' needs.

If you work in an organization, you may be asked to advise, or take part in, steps to limit or ban smoking there. The current position appears to be that courts expect reasonable employers to take action to eliminate passive smoking by their colleagues (Batten, 1992). All new workplaces in Europe are now required to provide separate rest rooms for smokers and non-smokers, or ban smoking completely. Existing workplaces have 3 years to do the same. People who smoke may be offered counselling, and may feel victimized and angry, especially if policies are implemented crudely (Batten, 1992).

STATUTORY REGISTRATION, *See* Professionalism

STRESS (*See also*: Journal, Supervision, Support groups, Thoughts)

The word stress is often used to refer to the situation which causes unwanted bodily reactions. It is clearer if the situation as perceived by the stressed person is called the *stressor*, while the word *stress* is used for the effects on the person.

What is stressful varies from person to person. Mild stimulation for one person is intolerable for another. It is the interaction of the potential source of stress with the perception of the individual, plus their attitude and physiological vulnerabilities, that matters. It is therefore a body–mind–body interaction, i.e. the receptors of the body receive the stimuli, the mind interprets the stimuli and the body reacts to these interpretations.

Stress is not entirely negative; some stressors can be beneficial, for example, they can lessen boredom, while stress may help a person to face up to themselves, to sort out their lives and develop new talents. Some stress if looked at positively may be exciting, while looked at negatively it would be anxiety-provoking. The mental attitude is important in the way we regard potential stress.

When a person is over-stressed, there may be effects on thinking, emotions, and the body. Thoughts often become more negative. Some people become anxious, others angry and others depressed, but in all these moods there are usually associated negative thoughts about self, others, or a particular situation. At the same time, the autonomic nervous system stimulates the body to produce signs of stress and again these vary between individuals. The heart rate becomes faster, the breathing more shallow, the digestive system slows down and muscles tense. Often a person feels tired but may not be able to sleep, while in others the opposite is true and they sleep too much. The results of all these changes may cause the person to become irritable or ill, or turn to unhealthy sources of comfort e.g. too much food, or smoking.

COPING WITH STRESS (*See also*: Assertiveness, Boundaries, Emotions, Journal, Post-Traumatic Stress Disorder, Self-awareness, Supervision, Support groups, Thoughts)

Often it is hard to realize that you

are over-stressed. It is only when they become ill that most people realize that something is wrong and even then they may regard the illness as something outside their control. The first step in overcoming stress is often understanding its very nature. After this it is a matter of seeing which of the three components of stress you can most readily or usefully alter: the stressor, your mind and/or your body.

The stressor my be altered, modified or eliminated, but sometimes just help in understanding it may be beneficial. For your mind, counselling or therapy, particularly cognitive therapy, silent prayer or meditation may help sort out negative thoughts, attitudes and perceptions and so generally improve your mental state; while for your body, exercise, relaxation and breathing exercises can all be beneficial. It is advantageous if you use coping strategies for both your body and your mind; if they are relaxed and in harmony, you are better able to cope with the stressors of life.

Effective coping with stress involves:

1. noticing your own *early* signs of too much stress, and taking action;
2. finding strategies that suit you, and using a variety of strategies.

As in counselling, small steps and gradual change are more likely to succeed for most people. It may also help to believe – really believe – that in counselling and the health professions generally, there is always more to do, and that it is up to each of us to set our own boundaries. Proper rest and recovery time is part of being an effective counsellor. Useful sources are Bond (1986), Burnard (1991), Fontana (1989), and Nichols (1993, Chapter 7).

SUED, BEING (*See also*: Codes of ethics, Insurance, Marketing)

Like all professionals, counsellors are legally required to exercise 'reasonable care and skill' in their work. 'Reasonable' is defined by the profession itself in its codes of ethics, major textbooks and the views of leading practitioners or (in a profession, like counselling, in which there is much disagreement) a **subgroup** of responsible practitioners within the profession (Cohen, 1992). Cohen further remarks that 'In theory, the courts are entitled to find that an established professional practice is itself negligent; in practice, particularly in medical negligence cases, they have been most reluctant to do so . . .' (p. 12). That is, the professions are trusted by the courts to set and maintain reasonable standards and methods.

The following advice seems clear from Cohen's discussion:

1. Do not guarantee improvement (or non-deterioration) to a client.
2. Do not give advice to clients.
3. Be sure that any information given is accurate and that 'homework' assignments are both legal and ethical.
4. Check your office for physical dangers (slippery floors, sharp edges, etc.) – 'reasonable care' again.
5. Recommend seeing a doctor if you suspect that the client's emotional problems may be physically caused.

All these actions, apart perhaps from (4), are part of normal professional practice by counsellors anyway. Failure or negligence even for these actions is unlikely, according to Cohen (1992), to lead to being sued but he emphasizes that much of the law in this area is unclear at present (*See also* Bond, 1993a).

SUICIDE

Comer (1992, p. 327) suggests that there are many myths about suicide, e.g.:

- It isn't true that people who talk about suicide, never commit it. People who commit suicide often give clues or definite warnings about their intention.
- People who attempt suicide are not necessarily fully intent on dying. Most are undecided about living or dying and sometimes 'gamble with death', leaving it to others or 'fate' to save them. They may not be aware of their motives.
- Apparent improvement doesn't mean the risk of suicide is over. Many suicides occur some months after apparent recovery from a suicidal crisis and when the person has the energy to act.
- People are not 'suicidal people' as such, they are people who want to kill themselves, but are suicidal only for a limited time.
- People who commit suicide don't necessarily have a mental disorder, but do tend to be extremely depressed.

People who threaten to commit suicide are typically in a state of overwhelming anguish, highly emotional and ambivalent, absorbed in interpersonal problems. They frequently experience rejection or loss and hostility towards self and others. They tend to think in unusually constricted ways that lead them to see suicide as the only logical answer to their problems.

GUIDELINES FOR INTERVENING

Approaches to helping people who threaten suicide vary according to whether it is primarily preventive or crisis intervention, i.e. after suicide has been attempted. If a client mentions suicide it needs to be taken seriously and talked about with the client straight away. Some clients may, however, only hint at suicide, so it is necessary to listen carefully for clues and confront the client gently; e.g. 'It sounds like you feel life isn't worth living for you and you want to end it'. If they ask if there is anything to live for, acknowledge the truth of this for them, and then ask if they will give you a chance to listen to them, talk about their feelings and find out if there is anything for them to live for.

Most approaches to preventing suicide suggest various tasks and stages, and assume you will be relatively active and directive.

1. Establish a positive relationship.
2. Clarify the problem.
3. Assess the risk.
   (a) Precipitating factors. Identify possible stressful events and

assess whether the level of stress is chronic or acute, recent, episodic or longer term.

(b) Symptoms. Assess the severity of symptoms and whether there has been any sharp, noticeable and sudden onset, e.g. severe depression, withdrawal, delusions, hallucinations, etc.

(c) Suicide plan. Assess the degree of detail and clarity of any plan. Does the client know when, where and how they intend to kill themselves, and in particular how specific is the intended timing and how lethal and realistic is the proposed method?

(d) History of suicide or depression.

(e) Clients' resources. Assess the nature and level of social support and the client's ability to make use of it. Explore the client's view of what other people think of them. A lack of sympathy or understanding can increase the risk of suicide.

4. Plan of action. Try to help the client see the temporary nature of the crisis and to recognize possible alternatives to suicide. Counsellors are typically more active/directive than usual, offering guidance and suggestions. Although many clients will view themselves as helpless most will have some strengths and resources, e.g. being employed. Initial plans need to be short-term

– identifying any potential 'low' spots in the day and ways of coping differently with them. Some counsellors negotiate a 'no-suicide pact' in which clients promise not to attempt suicide before the next counselling session, or before contacting you.

The strategy you choose depends partly on the degree of suicidal risk. If there is a high risk that a client may actually commit suicide then it may be necessary to refer for treatment, hospitalization, inform a GP, friends or relatives. Such action may mean breaking confidentiality. In this instance counsellors normally try to encourage the client to take the particular course of action for themselves; failing that, they ask the client's permission or agreement, and in the last resort simply tell the client what they are going to do before they do it. It can be helpful for the counsellor to tell the client that they don't want to carry the responsibility of the knowledge alone.

For most counsellors dealing with seriously suicidal clients, it is desirable to contact your supervisor as soon as possible. It is also essential to keep detailed case notes of the assessment, decisions or action taken with supporting evidence, together with times and dates, i.e. to act in a considered and professional way. See Bond (1993a, 1993c) for further discussion.

SUITABILITY OF CLIENTS FOR BRIEF COUNSELLING, See Assessment, Contraindications

SUMMARIES AND 'MOVING INTERVIEWS FORWARD' (*See also:* Challenge, Concreteness, Counselling, Hunch, Paraphrasing, Questions)

A summary of what your client has said is intended to help clarify what they mean, feel and think, and to make more sense of it. In addition it may increase your client's sense of control and hope, or reduce a feeling of being overwhelmed. Summaries need to be tentative (they may be wrong in content or emphasis), and have a flavour of 'This is where we are so far, in outline, so where next?'. 'Where next' may be further exploration, a focus on one problem or aspect of a problem, or the end of counselling. Gilmore (1973) discusses ways of offering clients a way forward, e.g. you might add a question to your summary, something like 'Is there one of these you'd like to talk about first?' This may be a different choice from your own! Or you might offer a hunch: 'Perhaps your main worry is . . .' or 'What seems to be most important is . . .' Alternatively, you might suggest focusing first on something which seems relatively straightforward (Gilmore, 1973).

A further variation is to add a hypothetical question to your summary. Gilmore (1973) calls this 'requesting a contrast'. For example, you might say, in the preliminary summary: 'You're unhappy about your work, especially whether you can cope with your boss's bullying. You'd love to be fitter and sleep better. And you're worried about being late for work, both because it lets your colleagues down and because being on time matters to you'. (Pause for your client to respond if he or she wishes.) A 'contrast' for this client would be to add: 'Suppose you were sleeping well. Do you think any of your other problems might look different?'

Requesting a contrast works very well sometimes: it helps a client clarify a present feeling or focus on a key point. The risks though are also potent: it can look like or become premature problem-solving (the instant solution) or lead to a general speculative discussion. Again, how you say it, and your attitude and general approach, are central, and, there is a strong artistic element. Timing, how you speak, and the quality of the relationship between you, all play a part.

A final variation is to ask your clients to summarize (sometimes!).

SUPERVISION (*See also:* Codes of ethics, Peer supervision, Process, Supervisors, BAC recognized, Tape-recorders, Transference)

In the UK, all counsellors are required to discuss their work regularly with a third party, the supervisor. This is primarily for addressing the needs of the client, but it is also for support of the counsellor. In addition the relationships between counsellor and client, and counsellor and supervisor, and the supervisor's 'process' all need to be kept in mind (Figure 3). A useful resource to work with, as it shows much of what actually happened in the session, not just what is reported, is a tape of a counselling session.

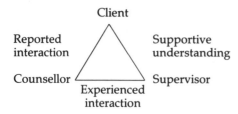

Figure 3 The process of supervision

Supervision is preferably carried out by someone who does not have another role (e.g. line manager) with the counsellor, and who therefore can concentrate solely on the counselling. The BAC Code of Ethics and Practice for the Supervision of Counsellors covers the nature of supervision, issues of responsibility, issues of competence, the management of supervision work and confidentiality.

Hawkins and Shohet (1989) distinguish several styles of supervision which may be used together or at different times, although they say that supervisors often have one preferred area of working. These different styles are as follows:

1. Reflect on what the client said and did, avoiding premature theorizing.
2. Explore the strategies and interventions used by the counsellor, and possible alternatives.
3. Explore the counselling process and relationship.
4. Focus on the counsellor's countertransference.
5. Focus on the 'here-and-now' process as reflecting aspects of the counselling itself.
6. Focus on the supervisor's or supervision group's countertransference.

Different ways of carrying out supervision are described in the BAC Code of Ethics for Supervisors:

1. **One-to-one: Supervisor–Counsellor.** This is the usual form of supervision, where the supervisor is more experienced than the counsellor and may also have attended a supervision course, or be recognized by BAC as a supervisor.
2. **One-to-one: Co-supervision.** Here the time is divided evenly between the two and they supervise each other. This method is only suitable for experienced counsellors and supervisors.
3. **Group supervision with a supervisor.** There is a range of ways of doing this from the supervisor working with each individual in turn, to the supervisor being the overall facilitator of a group process.
4. **Peer group supervision.** This is for a group of counsellors of similar experience working with each other.

See Houston (1990), Inskipp and Proctor (1989), Bond (1993a) and Horton (1993).

SUPERVISION, PRESENTING CLIENTS FOR (*See also:* Assessment, Contract, Crisis counselling, First impressions, Process, Working alliance).

Supervision sessions tend to go better when counsellors have spent some time preparing their presentations, and when a contract has been negotiated between counsellor and supervisor about, for example, length of sessions, frequency of sessions, fees, confidentiality and use of tape-recorders. Once this is done, there needs also to be some clear agreement about how you can best use the supervision time.

In presenting a client for supervision it is often useful to decide whether to focus on the entire counselling process, on only parts of it, on the client and his or her problems, or on your own sense of effectiveness and well-being. If, for example, you find a particular client difficult or challenging, you might want to present and discuss the difficulties you experience as issues in themselves, rather than specifically to do with a certain client. For example, a client who talks very little raises problems about how you might be more encouraging or inviting, and how you react when this happens.

As suggestions, we offer two 'schemes' for the presentation of clients. You may want to adopt one or other of them, or a combination of the two, or your own scheme after discussion with your supervisor. The important thing is that both you and your supervisor have a sense of purpose, and share some common ground on what kinds of issues or themes are suitable as case material for discussion. This goes for supervision either in a group or individually.

SCHEME ONE

This is a simple series of 'prompts' which offers ways of focusing on your feelings and thoughts about your relationships with your clients. They are meant as guidelines rather than rules.

1. What do I wish to accomplish through presenting this case?
2. What specific difficulties do I experience with this client?
3. Does this client remind me of aspects of myself and what do I think and feel about those aspects?
4. What does this client hope to accomplish in counselling?
5. What am I doing well with this client?
6. What could I do better with this client?
7. What am I learning about myself as a person and as a counsellor from this client?

SCHEME TWO

Presenting clients: Some frameworks for supervision and 'case' study (modified from Horton, 1993).

1. **Identification**
(a) First name only. Gender. Age/life stage.
(b) Your first impressions, client's physical appearance.
2. **Antecedents**
(a) How the client came to see you, e.g. self-referred.
(b) Context, e.g. agency, private practice, hospital clinic.
(c) What you knew about the client before you first met. How you used this information. Any existing relationship with the client and possible implications.

3. **Presenting problem and contract**
(a) Summary of presenting problem.
(b) Your initial assessment. Duration of problem. Precipitating factors (i.e. why the client came at this point). Current issues.
(c) Contract, e.g. frequency, length and number of sessions.

4. **Questions for supervision**
(a) Key issues.

5. **Focus on content**
(a) Description of the client in Gilmore's (1973) framework:
   (i) Work – significant activities, interests.
   (ii) Relationships – significant people.
   (iii) Identity – feelings and attitudes towards self.

Further possible elements are the implications of cultural, economic, social, political and other systems, and the client's early experiences, strengths and resources, beliefs, values, hopes, fears and fantasies.

(b) Problem definition
   (i) Construct a picture of the client's view of the present problem.
   (ii) What would the client like to happen, how would the client like things to be.
(c) Assessment – how you account for and explain the presenting problem
   (i) Any patterns/themes/connections?
   (ii) Which theoretical concepts/models apply? Hunches? New perspectives?
(d) Counselling plan
   (i) Direction or focus for future work?

(ii) Criteria for change?
(iii) Review and/or formulate plan(s).

6. **Focus on process**
(a) Strategies and interventions
   (i) What strategies and interventions have you used?
   (ii) What was your intention?
   (iii) What was their impact on the client?
   (iv) What alternative strategies are there?
(b) Relationship
   (i) What was happening between you and the client? Reframe the relationship; try a metaphor.
   (ii) What was happening within the client (transference)?
   (iii) What was happening within you (counter-transference)?
   (iv) What changes have there been in the relationship?
   (v) Evaluate the 'working alliance'.

7. **Focus on parallel process**
(a) What is happening between you and the supervisor?
(b) Any parallels with you and the client?

8. **Critical incident analysis**
(a) Description
   (i) What did client say and do at the particular point?
   (ii) What did you say and do?
   (iii) How did the client respond?
   (iv) What was happening within you?
(b) Analysis
   (i) What was happening within the client?
   (ii) What was going on between you and the client?
   (iii) Intention and impact of interventions/responses.

(iv) What hunches/hypotheses did you have at the time? And now?

(v) Review.

9. **Listening to aspects of covert communication**

(a) What was happening within you?

(i) How well did you listen to your own emotional response to a client?

(ii) You may be aware of your feelings first and thoughts later, or the reverse.

(iii) What did the client do and say to make you feel the way you did?

(iv) What does the client want from you and what sort of feeling is she or he trying to arouse in you to get it?

(b) What was happening within the client? Observe and reflect back when appropriate:

(i) Changes in voice quality – which might indicate an inner focus on something that is being seen or felt differently.

(ii) Idiosyncratic words or phrases.

(iii) Aspects of content you don't understand; perhaps the client doesn't either.

(iv) Encoded statements about other people or situations which may, at some level, be about the client: e.g. Client says: 'It upset me to see the little dog was alone.' A reformulation might be: 'Seeing the dog gave you a sense of desolation and rejection. Something about loneliness worries you' (Rice, 1980, p. 144). Reformulations can be practised almost as a game in supervision.

(vi) Disguised communication. Anything said about something out there *may* be about you and/ or the counselling relationship (Langs, 1982).

(vi) Non-verbal communication: e.g. silence, gazing into space, posture.

SUPERVISORS, BAC RECOGNIZED

All counsellors in the UK are required to have regular supervision so that they can discuss their work. Many experienced counsellors are also supervisors, and some of these have been assessed in the British Association for Counselling (BAC) recognition of supervisors scheme. This involves submitting a curriculum vitae with additional details of educational background and professional qualifications, counselling experience, training in supervision, supervision experience and reasons for requesting recognition. A tape of a supervision session is also submitted with commentaries by both the supervisor and the supervisee. If all these items reach the required standard, the supervisor is invited to a viva where they supervise another applicant and also act as supervisee.

SUPPORT, *See* Empathy, Common factors, Frameworks, Respect

SUPPORT GROUPS, PEER (*See also*: Boundaries, Contract, Stress)

The following ideas about peer support are adapted from Bond (1986) and Nichols and Jenkinson (1991). There are three sections: aims, guidelines and practical issues.

AIMS

The main purposes of peer support groups are:

1. to offer support to each member of the group by, for example, listening carefully to them, and
2. to receive support yourself.

Good support has been shown to reduce stress and lessen the risk of mental and physical illness (e.g. Argyle, 1992; Duck, 1992), though of course other methods are effective too. Support groups are not encounter groups or for therapy, or for attempting to solve other people's problems for them. They are for each person to talk as openly as they feel comfortable with about important concerns and worries.

GUIDELINES

1. Confidentiality is vital. A strict interpretation is agreeing not to discuss what happens in your group outside the group with anyone, not even with another group member or the person concerned.
2. Bond (1986, Chapter 6) distinguishes between several kinds of support. The most relevant for peer support groups are listening (pp. 158–70), sharing factual information, sharing personal information, advice and encouragement (pp. 147–51).
3. The section on pitfalls in giving and receiving support (Bond, 1986, pp. 173–6) may also be useful. The pitfalls include refusing support when you need it, feeling obliged to take unnecessary support, and choosing the wrong kind of support.
4. At the end of each meeting, review what is going on in the group, your reactions and if you would like to change anything.

PRACTICAL ISSUES

- How many people? (3–6)
- How often will you meet? (No accepted right amount. Weekly?)
- For how long? (Try 1 hour? And an initial contract of say 6 meetings?).
- Where will you meet?
- When? (If you meet irregularly who will arrange it?)
- How will you structure each session and allocate time?
- Do you want one of the group to be the leader? Or take turns? Or?

If your group goes well and you feel ambitious for it, try reading Nichols and Jenkinson (1991).

T

TAPE-RECORDING

You may want to tape-record your sessions with some clients for training or supervision purposes, or as a means of self-monitoring. The most obvious ethical principle involved is to consult clients beforehand, and for their permission to be freely given. This means saying what the recording is for, who will listen to it, and what will happen to the tape once it has been used, and listening hard to the client's reaction. If the client gives permission, it is a good idea to check again at the end of the session.

Most clients have no objection to being tape-recorded, but some are very uneasy about it, and their wishes should, of course, be respected. Sometimes clients appreciate knowing they can switch off the tape at any point, and this possibility can be part of your agreement before recording begins. Another option is to give the tape or a copy to your client after you have finished with it, or to ask them to

bring a blank tape to record the session on. If you do this then you may also want to suggest waiting a few days before listening to it, and discussing where and how they will listen and the possible effects. You may also want to agree confidentiality, i.e. whether anyone else will hear the tape.

Dryden (1983) discusses two obstacles to recording sessions for supervision: 'over-concern for clients' and problems with operating tape-recorders. On the first he argues that clients are not psychologically damaged by being recorded, that the concern expressed by some counsellors reflects their own anxiety. On the second, he asks the person concerned what it would be like for them to present an audible tape for supervision.

On a practical note, a small, unobtrusive tape-recorder is probably better than a bulky one and 120 minute tapes mean no interruption of the usual 50 minutes. Very good small recorders can now be bought quite cheaply, but most benefit from an additional, external microphone placed between you and your client.

Tapes need to be kept securely. It is good practice to write on the tape such details as date, session number, and when it should be destroyed.

TAPES, SELF-HELP, *See* Books

TEA AND COFFEE, *See* Drinks/ refreshments

THEORIES (*See also*: Common factors, Frameworks, Integration and eclecticism)

Relatively little has been written on the nature of theories of counselling, and to date, there has been no thorough examination of what actually constitutes an adequate theory of counselling, though there are of course numerous theories and approaches. One question which arises is: do theories of *personality* provide adequate theoretical underpinning for counselling practice?

Personality is usually understood to represent those characteristics of a person that account for consistent patterns of behaviour. Although they recognize that all people are similar in some respects, theories of personality are particularly concerned with the ways in which people differ from one another. Pervin (1993) suggests that personality theories seek to explain the what, how and why of personality: stable characteristics, and possible genetic and environmental determinants of them, and motives. So a theory of personality might help counsellors

understand to what extent a particular emotional state is characteristic of a client, how it developed, why it is experienced in certain circumstances, the way it is expressed, and if and how change is possible.

Nelson-Jones (1985) suggests four elements of a theory of counselling:

1. An indication of basic assumptions.
2. An explanation of how both functional and dysfunctional feelings, thoughts and behaviour are acquired.
3. An explanation of how they are perpetuated or sustained.
4. Practical suggestions for changing and modifying dysfunctional feelings, thought and behaviour that are internally consistent with the preceding elements (p. 131).

This analysis of the elements of a theory is very similar to the elements of personality theory as outlined by Pervin. Those approaches to counselling which place little if any importance on the origin of psychological problems would be found lacking as a theory if the elements are accepted. However, there are problems with the idea: Nelson-Jones isn't explicit about what kind of basic assumptions, and the practical component is vague and provides no guidelines on the type or nature of practical suggestions for change and no criteria for internal consistency.

Mahrer (1989) offers a different view. He argues that a theory of psychotherapy (or counselling) is *not* the same as a theory of personality. Its components are different and so too are the issues and questions with which it deals, even though he recognizes that it may imply or give birth to a theory of psychotherapy. He identifies seven components of a theory of psychotherapy:

1. Useful material to be elicited from the client.
2. How and what to listen for.
3. Explanatory concepts to describe the client's presenting problem and targets for change.
4. Therapeutic goals and direction of change.
5. General and more specific principles of change.
6. Strategies, techniques and procedures.
7. Description of what strategies to use under what circumstances or conditions.

Although Mahrer develops his discussion of the various components of a theory in greater depth than has been found elsewhere in the literature, it is still difficult to arrive at a clear operational definition that satisfactorily distinguishes between several of the components. Unlike Nelson-Jones' model of a theory of counselling, it does very much more than restate the elements of a theory of personality, but it is hard to avoid the pitfalls that stem from having such a complex formulation for theory and practice.

Many other theorists also draw a sharp distinction between theories of personality and theories of counselling or psychotherapy, e.g. Frankel (1984), Franks (1984) and Goldfried (1982). In the context of integration and eclecticism, Beitman (1990) says that counselling is a practical endeavour,

intended to help people change and therefore its theories must be connected to practical goals. He is critical of all the efforts to develop theories of personality and the emphasis placed on explanatory frameworks of the origin of psychological difficulty. He argues that theories of counselling must pay greater attention to the process of change and the factors maintaining psychological difficulty.

There is currently a lot of interest in the integration of theories of counselling. However, without a clear analysis of what constitutes a theory it is difficult to know what it is that is being integrated. While there remains no specific template for the analysis of a theory, nevertheless the individual practitioner may find enough to guide their understanding and efforts to explicate the theory that underpins their own practice.

THERAPEUTIC ALLIANCE, *See* Working alliance

THOUGHTS (*See also:* Assertiveness, Challenging, Depression, Emotions, Interpersonal Process Recall, Self-awareness, Values)

Some counsellors and theories of counselling emphasize the role of thoughts – especially some irrational beliefs – in troublesome emotions and behaviour (e.g. Moorey, 1990; Barker, 1992). A central idea in this approach is that when we repeatedly tell ourselves something like 'I must not make mistakes', we are likely to become upset and demoralized. To avoid this self-defeating, harmful pattern, the following broad steps can be taken:

1. Detect an irrational belief.
2. Challenge it.
3. Replace it with a more realistic belief.
4. Act on the new belief.

For example, suppose you 'catch' yourself or a client believing 'I should be able to do everything well', and see this as explaining, or at least contributing to, feeling incompetent, upset and anxious. Then you can dispute this belief: does it really make sense? Does *anyone* do *everything* well? What is my evidence? Next you can try to replace it, for example by 'I like doing things well but I'm better at some things than others', or 'It's human to make some mistakes' – whatever contradicts the particular irrational belief most effectively. A further step is to consolidate the new belief through action, to behave as if it's true.

This approach to changing thoughts is very consistent with the assertiveness approach to Rights. The list of Rights in the entry on assertiveness contains irrational beliefs by implication, e.g. 'People ought to respect me' or 'I musn't make mistakes and it is catastrophic if I do'. However, it is probably important to find a person's own variations.

Counsellors have their own specialized irrational beliefs, e.g. variations of 'I must like all my clients', 'I should be effective with all my clients', 'Rogers or Ellis would help this client', and 'Because I'm a counsellor, I shouldn't get stressed, tired, depressed, or anxious'. A general principle is to treat 'musts' and 'shoulds' as desirable rather than imperative, and unmet desires as regrettable rather than deeply upsetting.

A related cognitive technique is 'thought-stopping'. Phillips (1978) describes it and two variations – silent ridicule and repulsion – using the example of being obsessed with someone, and wanting to escape. Thought-stopping is a fairly standard technique; the variations illustrate some of the creativity of the cognitive approach (and of our minds). As with other techniques, each of these works sometimes, or appears to, but little is known about why or when, or when they have a negative effect.

Thought-stopping can be separated into three stages:

1. Make a list of positive scenes and activities (to act as 'rewards').
2. Think the obsessive and unwanted thought.
3. As you begin step (2), shout STOP, or dig your nails into your hand, and then think of one of your pleasurable scenes or activities. Repeat several times a day.

'Silent ridicule' is thinking differently about whatever you are obsessed with, e.g. exaggerating a person's least attractive feature. Again, repetitive practice is needed. Repulsion is imagining the person covered in something you find repulsive. Some people are repelled by this kind of technique, seeing it as 'brainwashing' and superficial; others see the techniques as using imaginative power for self-control, and as worth trying for their economy, with other approaches in reserve.

TIME BOUNDARIES (*See also:* Boundaries, Endings, Sexual attraction, Stress)

There is considerable agreement that it is part of your professional responsibility to be ready to start a session on time, but less agreement about when to end. Some counsellors believe they should be careful to end within 30–60 seconds of the appointed time, and that this should be done without an apology, but simply stating to the client that the time is up (Langs, 1982). Others have a more flexible approach, ending each session when it feels appropriate to do so within the time constraints and circumstances for both counsellor and client. They argue that a rigid adherence to boundaries is based on little more than convention. Most counsellors, however, feel that it is important to try to bring a session to a natural close near to the time originally agreed with the client.

There are strong arguments in favour of paying attention to ending on time. Maintaining time boundaries by starting and ending each session promptly can symbolize containment, holding and reliability and provide a client with a sense of security and safety. Only if you keep reasonable time boundaries can clients learn to use the time that is available. It is quite common for clients to start talking about a significant issue towards the end of a session, or to make an apparently throw-away comment. This may be a test of their own courage or of

your reaction in the relative safety of the limited time available, knowing at some level of awareness that it is possible to avoid taking the issue too deeply, at least in that session. Alternatively, it may be an attempt to manipulate you to spend more time with them.

A small clock behind the client allows you to say when there are only 5 or 10 minutes left and in this way begin to work towards ending and avoid an abrupt halt. Especially with brief counselling, it can be useful to conclude a session with some form of review. You can summarize what has been achieved and what needs to be discussed further or invite your client to do so.

At the end of some sessions a client may still be very distressed. Some counsellors remain silent giving the client a few moments to recover. They believe that it is the client's responsibility and, therefore, that the client will learn to deal with distress in their own way. Other counsellors prefer to offer an attention-switching or celebratory exercise (Evison and Horobin, 1983), to help clients gain composure. An ideal situation would be to allow clients to sit quietly in another room until they feel ready to leave. In many settings, however, this is not possible.

TIME MANAGEMENT, *See* Assertiveness, Boundaries, Stress, Values

TOUCH (*See also:* Crying, Kissing)

Touch can be interpreted as caring, patronizing, threatening, sympathetic, dominant, sexual, intimate or afraid. Like most non-verbal communications, it is ambiguous. The ambiguity is reduced but probably not eliminated by knowing the kind of touch, the context, and the people involved.

A hug is sometimes a very unhelpful thing to do, because it can block awareness of feelings. It can be more useful to talk about a desire to touch than to initiate it. However, touch is also a very basic way of making contact (perhaps especially when it is not done as a technique), so the most helpful suggestions may be to be clear about your own attitudes to touch and to role-play reactions to being touched by a client.

It can also be revealing to ask for feedback about your handshake (probably from candid friends). **Intensity** of shake can be seen quite differently by the two people involved: bonecrusher, dead fish, or in between? **Duration** of handshake can affect impressions too. And both qualities – intensity and duration – seem relatively easy to check and change.

TRANSFERENCE (*See also:* Counselling, Counter-transference, Empathy, First impressions, Immediacy, Supervision)

Transference is the displacing of an emotion or attitude from one relationship to another. In psychoanalysis it is more specifically the transferring by the client of their feelings and attitudes towards other members of their family (usually the parents or guardians) to the counsellor. Indicators include inappropriate reactions, e.g. too intense, inconsistent or ambivalent. The counsellor is idealized, imitated or hated (Jacobs, 1988; Stewart, 1992). Freud developed the idea of using transference to discover more about the deeper emotional state and early conflicts of clients. An alternative approach is to try to prevent its development, and if it does develop, to challenge it, separating yourself from the person your client would like to believe you are. The argument here is that empathy reduces transference, and that transference is an important factor in only a few relationships, unless counsellor or therapist neutrality deliberately encourages it.

TRUST (*See also:* Boundaries, Contract, Contraindications, Empathy, Questions (personal), Respect, Transference)

Although some clients are very trusting right from the start, developing trust is usually a gradual process. Clients will have had mixed experiences of previous relationships, some will have been let down very badly, and for these clients trusting you will naturally take some time.

Once counselling is under way, clients may test you by revealing relatively safe, though perhaps negative, things about themselves, or sharing a secret with you. It is important to take these things seriously, and show that you can be trusted with them by being non-judgemental. Clients may also want to know personal details about you. Again, it is important to take these requests seriously, but how you answer will depend on your approach to counselling generally. You don't need to appear evasive or secretive even if you don't want to answer personal questions directly.

TYPE, *See* Psychological type

u

UNITED KINGDOM COUNCIL FOR PSYCHOTHERAPY (UKCP)

The UKCP grew out of the first Psychotherapy Conference organized by the British Association for Counselling at Rugby in 1982. Annual meetings were held between 1983 and 1989. The UK Standing Conference for Psychotherapy was inaugurated in 1989 with the formal adoption of a constitution and the election of officers and council members. The name was changed in 1993 to the UK Council for Psychotherapy. UKCP has a federal structure in which similar kinds of psychotherapy member organizations are grouped together in sections, the largest of which are the Analytic, Humanistic and Integrative sections. Applications for full membership may be made by organizations significantly involved with the practice or teaching of psychotherapy. There is no individual membership. As 'Friends of the Council', BAC is in a special category of its own.

The essential aims of UKCP are stated as the protection of the public by the promotion of appropriate standards for training, research, education and the practice of psychotherapy. UKCP is clearly concerned with safeguarding and promoting the interests of the profession and its practitioners. It intends to set up appropriate structures as the representative body for psychotherapy in the UK. In 1993 UKCP launched its first national register of psychotherapists.

UKCP
c/o Regent's College
Inner Circle, Regent's Park
London NW1 4NS
UK

Tel: 071-487 7554

UNCONDITIONAL POSITIVE REGARD, *See* Respect

V

VALIDATION, OF COUNSELLOR EDUCATION/TRAINING COURSES IN THE UK

Public organizations such as Universities, Colleges and Institutes of Higher Education usually have some form of internal board or academic standards committee to validate their courses. They subject them to often rigorous procedures, annual audits and reports from external examiners who are independent of the course as well as to more extensive triennial reviews and major re-validation events every 5 or 6 years. Procedures vary, but validation events, often lasting a whole day, involve a panel of internal people not involved with the course or the department in question, together with external advisers who have knowledge and experience of counselling.

The panel and advisers interview the staff team and consider substantial documentation on the background of the course, selection and admission criteria and procedures, course organization and structure, staff CVs and, for each module or component of the course, the aims and objectives, methods of teaching and learning, content and methods of assessment and indicative reading. The usual academic criteria are employed and although panels will take recommendations from the external expert advisers, very seldom if ever do they require the course to satisfy professional criteria, e.g. for clinical supervision.

Increasingly, courses run by colleges, institutions and nowadays even private organizations are seeking University validation. Some courses also look to outside professional organizations for some kind of validation.

VALUES

One emphasis in counselling can be to help clients clarify what is most important to them. Someone who is relatively clear about their values is more able to make decisions, and perhaps less stressed (at least about values and decisions) as a result. If a client decides, for example, that being fit is less important at this time in her life than, say, a larger house, or vice versa, then she can use her time and energy accordingly.

The assumptions here are that it is not possible to do everything well, that there is always more to do, that priorities therefore need to be chosen, and that values are a good basis for choosing them. A further assumption is that it is desirable for values to be reflected in behaviour. Each person decides, deliberately or by default, whether to act on their values sufficiently or not.

Some key questions about values are:

- What are your main values?
- Do you act on them?
- Do you want to act on any of them more?
- If you do, what will you do less of?
- Do any of your values conflict with each other?
- How do your values affect others?

One of the most widely used systems of values is the Rokeach Value Survey (1973), but Schwartz's (1992) theory and measure may be replacing it.

VICTIM, *See* Drama Triangle

VIDEO, *See* Tape-recording

VIOLENCE AND ITS PREVENTION
(*See also:* Anger, Assertiveness, Empathy, Office, Paraphrasing, Touch)

Although the risk of violence is small,

preventive steps are worthwhile. We suggest the following:

1. Whenever possible avoid working in a building alone with a client, especially in the evenings or in buildings located away from a main public thoroughfare. In this situation maintain a strict appointment service and do not operate a drop-in clinic. If possible tell the caretaker that you will be working alone and when you expect to finish, but certainly inform a colleague or friend.

2. If you make a home visit, inform a colleague or friend where you are going and the time you expect to return.

3. Have a readily accessible telephone and consider having an alarm or 'panic' button installed in your counselling room. Carry a personal security device in situations in which you feel vulnerable.

4. If you suspect danger it may be advisable to cancel the appointment or, if actually working with a client, to bring the session to a close.

5. When working with a client of the opposite sex, try to ensure that someone of the same sex as the client is within calling range.

6. Take particular care with arrangements to work with any clients who have a psychiatric history involving acting out any form of violence or aggression.

7. Some counsellors consider it advisable and good practice to avoid any form of physical contact with a client apart from a handshake.

8. Calmness *and* empathy; sometimes calmness alone infuriates someone further.

Davies (1988) also considers the role of attitudes, e.g. 'I must never run away', and what he calls 'second order skills', e.g. the ability to take personal responsibility for your safety (an aspect of assertiveness) and the ability to analyse aggressive incidents. At an organizational level, there should be a system for recording and following up violent incidents, and support for those attacked. As well as physical injury, they may feel guilty or incompetent. Support could include, for example, counselling, paid leave or help with legal action.

Davies (1988) and Burns (1993) discuss managing and preventing violence. Wykes (1994) is an edited book on the incidence of violence towards several professional groups as well as its prevention and legal implications. There is little research so far on the effectiveness of the strategies outlined above.

W

WARMTH (*See also:* Emotions, Love, Paraphrasing, Readiness to change, Respect, Sexual feelings)

Warmth and being affectionate are the opposite of distant or aloof. They imply a liking for people, and a caring approach, especially with people who are distressed or confused. Warmth, however, is not necessarily something you will always feel or feel equally for every client, and some clients are likely to experience you as warmer than do other clients. Warmth, like trust, is often a process rather than something established immediately, as the expression 'to warm to somebody' implies. It helps if you have an open and inviting attitude towards clients when you first meet them, and to allow yourself time to get to know them, and them to get to know you.

Excessive warmth can be as much of a problem as no warmth at all. Some clients may feel overpowered or uncomfortable if you are warm towards them. It can be very difficult for clients to express angry feelings towards you, for example, if you allow your natural warmth to spill over into being too protective or over-friendly. Similarly, clients can feel reticent about expressing what they think of as their negative aspects if they feel they might risk your withdrawal of affection from them. This might have very strong echoes of the past for many clients. And some clients prefer a formal, business-like approach.

WORKING ALLIANCE (*See also:* Contract, Core conditions, Counselling, Rapport)

Jacobs (1988), a psychodynamic counsellor, writes: 'The working relationship that exists between counsellor and client (sometimes known as the working alliance) is essentially one of adult meeting with adult, not simply as two equal human beings, who share the problems of living, but also as two people who meet to work together on a problem or set of problems. Individual counselling involves an implicit agreement between two adults (counsellor and client) to cooperate in trying to understand certain less adult and less mature aspects in one of them' (p. 99). This definition reflects (i) the psychodynamic emphasis on insight rather than goals, and (ii) the fact that counselling is dedicated to a particular set of purposes, and isn't simply a problem-sharing exercise between two people who have the same needs from the relationship. This sense of purpose needs to be communicated by all counsellors, whatever their approach to counselling. It also needs to be accepted by clients. The initial interview, if handled properly, can go a long way towards establishing a purposeful and concentrated atmosphere in which you work together on the concerns of the client.

WRITING (*See also:* Freewriting, Journals, Professionalism, Research)

We would like to encourage practitioners to consider writing up their ideas for professional journals. One obstacle is the myth that writers find writing easy; most rewrite many times, and regard writing as (at least in part) a punishing process. However, writing also helps clarify thoughts and may help others, and there are techniques to try when inspiration fails, e.g. freewriting; reading your material aloud (or – particularly brave – asking someone else to); writing a detailed outline; writing as if to a friend. Burnard (1992), Turk and Kirkman (1989), and Becker (1986) offer views, research findings and advice.

ZEST, MAINTAINING, *See* Assertiveness, Burnout, Journal, Referral, Self-awareness, Stress, Support groups

References

Adams, K. (1990) *Journal to the Self: 22 Pathways to Personal Growth*, Warner Books, New York.

Alladin, W.J. (1993) Ethnic matching in counselling, in *Questions and Answers on Counselling in Action* (ed. Dryden, W.), Sage, London.

Allinson, T., Cooper, C.L. and Reynolds, P. (1989) Stress counselling in the workplace. The Post Office experience. *The Psychologist*, **2**(9), 384–88.

Aronson, E. (1992) *The Social Animal*, 6th edn, Freeman, New York.

Argyle, M. (1992) *The Social Psychology of Everyday Life*, Routledge, London.

Aveline, M. and Dryden, W. (eds) (1988) *Group Therapy in Britain*, Open University, Milton Keynes.

Barker, C. (1985) Interpersonal process recall in clinical training and research, in *New Developments in Clinical Psychology* (ed. Watts, F.N.), BPS/Wiley, Chichester, UK.

Barker, P.J. (1992) *Severe Depression. A practitioner's guide*, Chapman & Hall, London.

Barker, P.J. (1993) *A Self Help Guide to Managing Depression*. Chapman & Hall, London.

Barkham, M. (1990) Research in individual therapy, in *Individual Therapy. A Handbook* (ed. Dryden, W.), Open University, Milton Keynes.

Barkham, M. (1993a) Understanding, implementing and presenting counselling evaluation, in *Counselling and Psychology for Health Professionals* (eds Bayne, R. and Nicolson, P.), Chapman & Hall, London.

Barkham, M. (1993b) Research and practice, *Questions and Answers on Counselling in Action* (ed. Dryden, W.), Sage, London.

Barrett-Lennard, G.T. (1993) The phases and focus of empathy. *British Journal of Medical Psychology*, **66**, 3–14.

Batten, L. (1992) Stubbing out passive smoking, *Personnel Management*, August, 24–7.

Bayne, R. (1993) Psychological type, conversations and counselling, in *Counselling and Psychology for Health*

Professionals (eds Bayne, R. and Nicolson, P.), Chapman & Hall, London.

Bayne, R. (1994) The 'Big Five' versus the MBTI. *The Psychologist*, 7(1), 14–16.

Becker, H.S. (1986) *Writing for Social Scientists. How to start and finish your thesis, book or article*, University of Chicago Press, Chicago.

Beitman, B.D. (1990) Chapter 3, in *Eclect-icism and Integration in Counselling and Psychotherapy* (eds Dryden, W. and Norcross, J.C.), Gale Centre Publications, Loughton, UK (081-5089344).

Benjamin, A. (1969) *The Helping Interview*, Houghton Mifflin, Boston.

Bergin, A. and Garfield, S. (1994) *Handbook of Psychotherapy and Behaviour Change*, 4th edn, John Wiley, Chichester.

Bimrose, J. (1993) Counselling and social context, in *Counselling and Psychology for Health Professionals* (eds Bayne, R. and Nicolson, P.), Chapman & Hall, London.

Bloch, S. (1982) *What is Psychotherapy*, Oxford University Press, Oxford.

Bond, M. (1986) *Stress and Self-Awareness: A Guide for Nurses*, Heinemann, London.

Bond, T. (1993a) *Standards and Ethics for Counselling in Action*, Sage, London.

Bond, T. (1993b) Counsellor/client sex, in *Questions and Answers on Counselling in Action* (ed. Dryden, W.), Sage, London.

Bond, T. (1993c) When to protect the client from self-destruction, *Questions and Answers on Counselling in Action* (ed. Dryden, W.), Sage, London.

Bond, T. (1993d) Reporting a colleague's misconduct, in *Questions and Answers*

on Counselling in Action (ed. Dryden, W.), Sage, London.

Brammer, L.M., Abrego, P.J. and Shostrom, E. (1993) *Therapeutic Counseling and Psychotherapy*, 6th edn, Prentice Hall, Englewood Cliffs, NJ.

Brenner, D. (1982) *The Effective Psycho-therapist*, Pergamon, Oxford.

British Association for Counselling (1988, 1990b) The Recognition of Counsellor Training Courses, BAC, Rugby.

British Association for Counselling (1990a) *The Code of Ethics and Practice for Counsellors*, BAC, Rugby.

British Association for Counselling (1993a) The Complaints Procedures – lessons from the past year. *Counselling*, February 14–15.

British Association for Counselling (1993b) The BAC Basic Principles of Counselling, *Counselling*, August, 155–6.

Budman, S.H. and Gurman, A.S. (1988) *Theory and Practice of Brief Therapy*, Guilford, London.

Bugental, J.F.T. and Bugental, E.K. (1980) The far side of despair, *Journal of Humanistic Psychology*, 20, 49–68.

Burnard, P. (1991) *Coping with Stress in the Health Professions*, Chapman & Hall, London.

Burnard, P. (1992) *Writing for Health Professionals*, Chapman & Hall, London.

Burns, J. (1993) Working with potential violence, in *Counselling and Psychology for Health Professionals* (eds Bayne, R. and Nicolson, P.), Chapman & Hall, London.

Chaplin, J. (1993) Women counselling women, in *Questions and Answers on*

Counselling in Action (ed. Dryden, W.), Sage, London.

Charles-Edwards, D., Dryden, W. and Woolfe, R. (1989) Professional issues in counselling, in *Handbook of Counselling in Britain* (eds Dryden, W. *et al.*), Tavistock/Routledge, London.

Clarke, K.M. Greenberg, L.S. (1986) Differential effects of the Gestalt two-chair intervention and problem-solving in resolving decisional conflict, *Journal of Counselling Psychology*, **33**(1), 11–15.

Clayton, P.J. and Barrett, J.E. (eds) (1983) *Treatment of Depression: Old Controversies and New Approaches*, Raven Press, New York.

Cohen, K. (1992) Some legal issues in counselling and psychotherapy. *British Journal of Guidance and Counselling* **20**(1), 10–26.

Comer, R.J. (1992) *Abnormal Psychology*, Freeman, New York.

Corey, G. (1991) *Theory and Practice of Counseling and Psychotherapy*, 4th edn, Brooks/Cole, Monterey, Pacific Grove, CA.

Corey, M. and Corey, G. (1992) *Groups: Process and Practice*, 4th edn, Brooks/Cole, Pacific Grove, CA.

Corey, M. and Corey, G. (1993) *Becoming a Helper*, 2nd edn, Brooks Cole, Pacific Grove, CA.

Cormier, W.H. and Cormier, L.S. (1991) *Interviewing Strategies for Helpers*, Brooks/Cole, Pacific Grove, CA.

d'Ardenne, P. (1993) Transcultural counselling and psychotherapy in the 1990s, *British Journal of Guidance and Counselling*, **21**(1), 1–7.

Dalton, P. (1992) Chapter 2, in *Hard-earned Lessons from Counselling in Action* (ed. Dryden, W.), Sage, London.

Davenport, R.B. and Pipes, D.S. (1990) *Introduction to Psychotherapy: Common Clinical Wisdom*, Prentice-Hall, London.

Davies, W. (1988) How not to get hit, *The Psychologist*, **2**(5), 175–6.

Deurzen Smith, E. van (1990) Existential therapy, in *Individual Therapy: A Handbook* (ed. Dryden, W.), Open University, Milton Keynes.

Deurzen Smith, E. van (1992) Counselling psychology in Europe, *Counselling Psychology Review*, **7**(3), 5–10.

Dickson, A. (1987) *A Woman in Your Own Right* (revised edn), Quartet London.

Dillon, J.T. (1990) *The Practice of Questioning*, Routledge, London.

Dinkmeyer, D. (1985) Adlerian Psychotherapy and Counseling, in *Contemporary Psychotherapies – models and methods* (eds S.J. Lynn and J.P. Garske), Merrill, London.

Draucker, C.B. (1992) *Counselling Survivors of Childhood Sexual Abuse*, Sage, London.

Dryden, W. (1983) Supervision of audio-tapes in counselling: obstacles to trainee learning, *The Counsellor*, **3**(8), 18–25.

Dryden, W. (ed.) (1985) *Therapist's Dilemmas*, Harper & Row, London.

Dryden, W. (ed.) (1990) *Individual Therapy: A Handbook*, Open University, Milton Keynes.

Dryden, W. (1991) *A Dialogue with Arnold Lazarus: 'It Depends'*, Open University, Milton Keynes.

Dryden, W. (ed.) (1992) *Hard Earned Lessons from Counselling in Action*, Sage, London.

Dryden, W. (ed.) (1993) *Questions and Answers on Counselling in Action*, Sage, London.

Dryden, W. and Feltham, C. (1992) *Brief Counselling: A Practical Guide for Beginning Practitioners*, Open University, Milton Keynes.

Dryden, W. and Norcross, J.C. (eds) (1990) *Eclecticism and Integration in Counselling and Psychotherapy*, Gale Centre Publications, Loughton, UK (081-508 9344).

Dryden, W. and Thorne, B. (1991) *Training and Supervision for Counselling in Action*, Sage, London.

Duck, S. (1992) *Human Relationships*, 2nd edn, Sage, London.

Edelstein, E.L., Nalthanson, D.L. and Stone, A.M. (eds) (1989) *Denial: A Clarification of Concepts and Research*, Plenum Press, New York.

Egan, G. (1975, 1990) *The Skilled Helper*, 1st and 4th edns, Brooks/Cole, Monterey.

Ekman, P. (1992) Are there basic emotions? *Psychological Review*, **99**(3), 550–53.

Ekman, P. (1993) Facial expression and emotion, *American Psychologist*, **48**(4), 384–92.

Elton Wilson, J. (1993) Towards a personal model of counselling, in *Questions and Answers on Counselling in Action*, (ed. Dryden, W.), Sage, London.

Ernst, S. and Goodison, L. (1982) *In Our Own Hands*, The Women's Press, London.

Evison, R. and Horobin, R. (1983) *How to Change Yourself and Your World*. Co-counselling Phoenix, Sheffield, England.

Eysenck, H.J. (1992) The outcome problem in psychotherapy, in *Psychotherapy and its Discontents*, (eds Dryden, W. and Feltham, C.), Open University, Milton Keynes, UK.

Feltham, C. (1993) Making a living as a counsellor, in *Questions and Answers on Counselling in Action*, (ed. Dryden, W.), Sage, London.

Feltham, C. and Dryden, W. (1993) *Dictionary of Counselling*, Whurr Publishers, London.

Fontana, D. (1989) *Managing Stress*, BSP/Routledge, London.

Foss, B. (1986) *Report for BAC on Accreditation Scheme*, BAC, Rugby.

Frank, J.D. (1981) Therapeutic components shared by all psychotherapies, in *Psychotherapy Research and Behaviour Change*, (eds Harvey, J.H. and Parks, M.M.), American Psychological Association, Washington DC.

Frankel, A.J. (1984) *Four Therapies Integrated*, Prentice Hall, Englewood Cliffs, New Jersey.

Franks, C.M. (1984) On conceptual and technical integrity in psychoanalysis and behaviour therapy. Two fundamentally incompatible systems, in *Psychoanalytic Therapy and Behaviour Change: is integration possible?* (eds Arkowitz, H. and Messer, S.B.), Plenum, New York and London.

Gallo, P.S. (1978) Meta-analysis – a mixed metaphor, *American Psychologist*, **33**(5), 515–17.

Garfield, S.L. (1989) *The Practice of Brief Psychotherapy*, Pergamon, Oxford.

Gendlin, E.T. (1981) *Focusing*, 2nd edn, Bantam, London.

Gilbert, P. (1992) *Counselling for Depression*, Sage, London.

Gilmore, S.K. (1973) *The Counselor-in-Training*, Prentice Hall, London.

Goldfried, M.R. (1982) *Converging Themes in Psychotherapy*, Springer, New York.

Green, H. (1964) *I Never Promised You a Rose Garden*, Pan, London.

Greenberg, L.S. and Safran, J.D. (1990) *Emotion in Psychotherapy*, Guilford Press, New York.

Hallam, R. (1992) *Counselling for Anxiety Problems*, Sage, London.

Hawkins, P. and Shohet, R. (1989) *Supervision in the Helping Professions*, Open University, Milton Keynes.

Hayes, S.C. and Melancon, S.M. (1989) Comprehensive distancing, paradox, and the treatment of emotional avoidance, in *Therapeutic Paradox*, (ed. Ascher, L.M.) Guildford Press, New York.

Heppner, P.P., Kivligham, D.M. and Wampold, B. (1992) *Research Design in Counseling*, Brooks/Cole, Pacific Grove, CA.

Hill, C.E. and Corbett, M.M. (1993) A perspective on the history of process and outcome research in counseling psychology. *Journal of Counselling Psychology*, **40**(1), 3–24.

Hopson, B. and Scally, M. (1981) *Lifeskills Teaching*, McGraw-Hill, Maidenhead.

Horton, I. (1993) Supervision, in *Counselling and Psychology for Health Professionals*, (eds Bayne, R. and Nicolson, P.), Chapman & Hall, London.

Houston, G. (1990) *Supervision and Counselling*, Rochester Foundation, 8 Rochester Terrace, London NW1.

Inskipp, F. (1993) Beyond Egan, in *Questions and Answers on Counselling in Action*, (ed. Dryden, W.), Sage, London.

Inskipp, F. and Proctor, B. (1989) *Counselling Skills for Supervision* (Audiotapes with notes and exercises), Alexia Publications, 2 Market Terrace, St. Leonards-on-Sea, East Sussex (also from BAC).

Ivey, A.E., Ivey, M.B. and Simek-Downing, L. (1987) *Counseling and Psychotherapy: Integrating skills, Theory and Practice*, 2nd edn, Prentice Hall, London.

Ivey, A.E., Ivey, M.B. and Simek-Morgan, L. (1993) *Counseling and Psychotherapy: A Multicultural Perspective*, 3rd edn, Allyn and Bacon, London.

Jacobs, M. (1988) *Psychodynamic Counselling in Action*, Sage, London.

Jeffers, S. (1991) *Feel the Fear and Do It Anyway*, Arrowbooks.

Kagan, N. (1984) Interpersonal Process Recall: Basic methods and recent research, in *Teaching Psychological Skills*, (ed. Larsen, D.) Brooks/Cole, Monterey, CA.

Karpman, S.B. (1968) Fairy tales and script drama analysis. *TA Bulletin*, *VII*(26), April, 39–43.

Lakoff, G. and Johnson, M. (1980) *Metaphors We Live By*, University of Chicago Press, London.

Lambers, E. (1993) When the counsellor shares the client's problem, in *Questions and Answers on Counselling in Action*, (ed. Dryden, W.) Sage, London.

Lancaster, B. (1991) *Mind, Brain and Human Potential*, Element, New York.

Lane, D. (1990) Counselling psychology in organisations. *The Psychologist*, **12**, 540–44.

Lang, G., Molen, H. van der, Trower, P. and Look, R. (1990) *Personal Conversations: Roles and Skills for Counsellors*, Routledge, London.

Langs, R. (1982) *Workbooks for Psychotherapists, Vol. II*, Listening and Formulating, Newconcept Press, Emerson, NJ.

Lasswell, M.E. and Lobsenz, N.M. (1980) *Styles of Loving*, Ballantine, New York.

Lebow, J.L. (1987) Developing a personal integration: Principles for model construction and practice. *Journal of Marital and Family Therapy*, **13**, 1–14.

Lee, J. (1988) Love-styles, in *The Psychology of Romantic Love* (eds Sternberg, R.J. and Barnes, M.C.), Yale University Press, London.

Levenson, R.W. and Ruef, A.M. (1992) Empathy: A physiological substrate *Journal of Personality and Social Psychology*, **63**(2), 234–46.

Lewis, C. (1993) Making use of research, in *Counselling and Psychology for Health Professionals*, (eds Bayne, R. and Nicolson, P.), Chapman & Hall, London.

Ley, P. (1988) *Communicating with Patients*, Croom Helm, London.

Loftus, E.F. (1993) The reality of repressed memories, *American Psychologist*, **48**(5), 518–37.

Loftus, E.F. and Loftus, G.R. (1980) On the permanence of stored information in the brain, *American Psychologist*, **35**, 409–20.

McKinney, K. (1990) Sexual harassment of University faculty, *Sex Roles*, **23**(7–8), 421–38.

McLeod, J. (1990) The client's experience of counselling and psychotherapy: a review of the research literature, in *Experiences of Counselling in Action* (eds Mearns, D. and Dryden, W.), Sage, London.

McNeilly, C. and Howard, K. (1991) The effects of psychotherapy: a re-evaluation based on dosage, *Psychotherapy Research*, **1**, 74–8.

Mahalik, J.R. (1990) Systematic eclectic models, *The Counseling Psychologist*, **18**(4), 655–79.

Mahrer, A.R. (1989) *The Integration of Psychotherapies*, Human Science Press, NY.

Mann, J. (1973) *Time Limited Psychotherapy*, Harvard University Press, Cambridge, MA.

Matek, O. (1988) Obscene phone callers. Special issue: The Sexually Unusual: Guide to Understanding and Helping, *Journal of Social Work and Human Sexuality*, **7**(1), 113–30.

Mearns, D. (1990a) The counsellor's experience of failure, in *Experiences of Counselling in Action* (eds Mearns, D. and Dryden, W.), Sage, London.

Mearns, D. (1990b) The counsellor's experience of success, in *Experiences of Counselling in Action* (eds Mearns, D. and Dryden, W.), Sage, London.

Mearns, D. (1992) Chapter 6, in *Hard-earned Lessons from Counselling in Action* (ed. Dryden, W.), Sage, London.

Mearns, D. (1993) Against indemnity insurance, in *Questions and Answers on Counselling in Action* (ed. Dryden, W.), Sage, London.

Mearns, D. and Thorne, B. (1988) *Person-Centred Counselling in Action*, Sage, London.

Merry, T. and Lusty, B. (1993) *What is Person-Centred Therapy?* Gale Publications, Loughton, UK (081-508 9344).

Mills, C.K. and Wooster, A.D. (1987) Crying in the counselling situation, *British Journal of Guidance and Counselling*, **15**(2), 125–30.

Moorey, S. (1990) Cognitive therapy, in *Individual Therapy: A Handbook* (ed. Dryden, W.), Open University, Milton Keynes.

Moos, R.H. (ed.) (1991) *Coping with Life Crises – an integrated approach*, Plenum, NY.

Morley, W.F., Messick, J.M. and Aguilera, D.C. (1967) Crisis, paradigms of intervention. *Journal of Psychiatric Nursing*, **5**, 537–8.

Mueller, J. (1983) Neuroanatomic correlates of emotions, in *Emotions in Health and Illness: Theoretical and Research Foundations*, eds Temoshok, L., Van Dyke, C. and Zegans, L.S., Grune and Stratton, Orlando, FL.

Murgatroyd, S. and Woolfe, R. (1982) *Coping with Crisis*, Harper and Row, London.

Murray, S. (1992) *PPS Practitioner Guide and Reference Book*, PPS, Standelene House, Kincardine, Alloa, Clacks FK10 4NX, UK.

Myers, I.B. (1980) *Gifts Differing*, Consulting Psychologists Press, Palo Alto, CA.

Nelson-Jones, R. (1984) *Personal Responsibility, Counselling and Therapy*, Harper and Row, London.

Nelson-Jones, R. (1985) Eclecticism, integration and comprehension in counselling theory, *British Journal of Guidance and Counselling*, **13**(2), 129–38.

Nichols, K.A. (1993) *Psychological Care in Physical Illness*, 2nd edn, Chapman & Hall, London.

Nichols, K.A. and Jenkinson, J. (1991) *Leading a Support Group*, Chapman & Hall, London.

Nicolson, P. and Bayne, R. (1990) *Applied Psychology for Social Workers*, 2nd edn, Macmillan, Basingstoke, UK.

Norcross, J.C. and Grencavage, L.M. (1989) Eclecticism and integration in counselling and psychotherapy: major themes and obstacles, in *Eclecticism and Integration in Counselling and Psychotherapy* (eds Dryden, W. and Norcross, J.C.), Gale Centre Publications, Loughton, UK (081-508 9344).

Novaco, R.W. (1975) *Anger Control*, Lexington Books, Lexington, MA.

Orford, J. (1992) *Community Psychology: Theory and Practice*, Wiley, Chichester, UK.

Ortony, A. and Turner, T.J. (1990) What's basic about basic emotions? *Psychological Review*, **97**(3), 315–31.

Parry, G. (1990) *Coping with Crises*, BPS/Routledge, London.

Patterson, C.H. (1984) Empathy, warmth and genuineness: a review of reviews. *Psychotherapy*, **21**(4), 431–8.

Peake, T.H., Borduin, C.M. and Archer, R.P. (1988) *Brief Psychotherapies – Changing Frames of Mind*, Sage, London.

Pennebaker, J.W. (1993) Putting stress into words: health, linguistic and therapeutic implications, *Behaviour Research and Therapy*, **31**(6), 539–48.

Pennebaker, J.W., Colder, M. and Sharp, L.K. (1990) Accelerating the coping process, *Journal of Personality and Social Psychology*, **58**(3), 528–37.

Pervin, L.A. (1993) *Personality Theory and Research*, 6th edn, Wiley, London.

Phillips, D. (1978) *How to Fall Out of Love*, Macdonald Futura, London.

Pipes, R.B., Schwartz, R. and Crouch, P. (1985) Measuring client fears, *Journal of Consulting and Clinical Psychology*, **53**(6), 933–4.

Prochaska, J.O. and DiClemente, C.C. (1984) *The Transtheoretical Approach*, Dow Jones Irwin, Homewood, IL.

Provost, J.A. (1984) *A Casebook: Applications of the Myers-Briggs Type Indicator in Counselling*, Center for Applications of Psychological Type, Gainesville, FL.

Rainer, T. (1978) *The New Diary*, St Martin's Press, NY.

Rakos, R. (1991) *Assertive Behaviour: Theory, Research and Training*, Routledge, London.

Raphael, B. (1984) *The Anatomy of Bereavement*, Hutchinson, London.

Reddy, M. (1987) *The Manager's Guide to Counselling at Work*, BPS/Methuen, London.

Rice, L.N. (1980) A client-centred approach to supervision, in *Psychotherapy Supervision: Theory, Research and Practice* (ed. Hess, A.K.), Wiley, New York.

Rogers, C.R. (1957) The necessary and sufficient conditions for therapeutic personality change, *Journal of Consulting Psychology*, **21**(2), 95–103.

Rogers, C.R. (1961) *On Becoming a Person*, Constable, London.

Rogers, C.R. (1973) *Encounter Groups*, Penguin, Harmondsworth, UK.

Rogers, C.R. (1980) *A Way of Being*, Houghton Mifflin, Boston, MA.

Rogers, C.R. (1987) Comments on the issue of equality in psychotherapy, *Journal of Humanistic Psychology*, **27**(1), 38–40.

Rogers, C.R. and Sandford, R.C. (1980) Client-Centred Psychotherapy, in *Comprehensive Textbook of Psychiatry*, eds Kaplan, H., Sadock, B. and Freeman, A., Vol 3, Williams and Wilkins, Baltimore.

Rokeach, M. (1973) *The Nature of Human Values*, Free Press, NY.

Rosen, G.M. (1981) Guidelines for the review of do-it-yourself treatment books, *Contemporary Psychology*, **26**(3), 190–91.

Rosen, G.M. (1987) Self-help treatment books and the commercialization of psychotherapy, *American Psychologist*, **42**(1), 46–51.

Rosenthal, R. (1990) How are we doing in soft psychology? *American Psychologist*, **45**, 775–7.

Rowan, J. (1983) *The Reality Game: A Guide to Humanistic Counselling and Psychotherapy*, Routledge, London.

Rowe, D. (1987) *Beyond Fear*, Fontana, London.

Russell, J.A. (1991) Culture and the categorization of emotions, *Psychological Bulletin*, **110**(4), 426–50.

Russell, J.A. (1993) *Out of Bounds: Sexual Exploitation in Counselling and Therapy*, Sage, London.

Schwartz, S.H. (1992) Universals in the content and structure of values: theoretical advances and empirical tests in 20 countries, *Advances in Experimental Social Psychology*, **25**, 1065.

Scott, M.J. and Stradling, S.E. (1992) *Counselling for Post-Traumatic Stress Disorder*, Sage, London.

Shaver, P.R. and Hazan, C. (1988) A biased overview of the study of love, *Journal of Social and Personal Relationships*, **5**(4), 473–501.

Sheffield, C.J. (1989) The invisible intruder: women's experience of obscene phone calls, *Gender and Society*, **3**(4), 483–8.

Shillito-Clarke, C. (1993) Book review, *Counselling*, August, 219.

Shlien, J.M. (1989) Boy's person-centred perspective on psycho-diagnosis – a response, *Person Centred Review*, **4**(2), 157–62.

Shohet, R. and Wilmot, J. (1991) The key issue in the supervision of counsellors: the supervisory relationship, in *Training and Supervision for Counselling in Action* (eds Dryden, W. and Thorne, B.), Sage, London.

Sternberg, R.J. and Barnes, M.C. (1988) *The Psychology of Romantic Love*, Yale University Press, London.

Stewart, I. (1989) *Transactional Analysis in Action*, Sage, London.

Stewart, W. (1992) *An A–Z of Counselling Theory and Practice*, Chapman & Hall, London.

Stiles, W.B., Shapiro, D.A. and Elliott, R. (1986) Are all psychotherapies equivalent? *American Psychologist*, **41**, 165–80.

Storr, A. (1990) *The Art of Psychotherapy*, 2nd edn, Heinemann/Secker and Warburg, London.

Sue, D.W. and Sue, D. (1990) *Counselling the Culturally Different: Theory and Practice*, 2nd edn, Wiley, London.

Sutherland, N.S. (1987) *Breakdown: A Personal Crisis and a Medical Dilemma*, Weidenfeld & Nicolson, London.

Tavris, C. (1984) On the wisdom of counting to ten. Personal and social dangers of anger expression, in *Review of Personality and Social Psychology* (ed. Shaver, P.), Vol. 5, Sage, London.

Tavris, C. (1989) *Anger: The Misunderstood Emotion*, 2nd edn, Touchstone Books/Simon & Schuster, London.

Templeman, T.L. and Sinnett, R.D. (1991) Patterns of sexual arousal and history in a 'normal' sample of young men, *Archives of Sexual Behaviour*, **20**, 137–50.

Townsend, R. (1984) *Further Up the Organisation*, Coronet Books, Hodder & Stoughton, Sevenoaks, UK.

Turk, C. and Kirkman, J. (1989) *Effective Writing: Improving Scientific, Technical and Business Communication*, 2nd edn, E. and F.N. Spon, London.

Walker, M. (1992a) *Surviving Secrets*, Open University, Milton Keynes.

Walker, M. (1992b) Chapter 10 (untitled), in *Hard-earned Lessons from Counselling in Action* (ed. Dryden, W.), Sage, London.

Walker, M. (1993) When values clash, in *Questions and Answers on Counselling in Action* (ed. Dryden, W.), Sage, London.

Webb, W.B. (1981) How to or not how to . . . , *Contemporary Psychology*, **26**, 192–3.

Whitaker, D.S. (1985) *Using Groups to Help People*, Routledge, London.

Woolfe, R. (1990) Counselling psychology in Britain: an idea whose time has come, *The Psychologist*, **12**, 531–5.

Woolfe, R., Dryden, W. and Charles-Edwards, D. (1989) The nature and range of counselling practice, in *Handbook of Counselling in Britain* (eds Dryden *et al.*), Tavistock/Routledge, London.

Worden, W.J. (1984) *Grief Counselling and Grief Therapy*, Tavistock, London.

Wortman, C.B. and Silver, R.C. (1989) The myths of coping with loss, *Journal of Consulting and Clinical Psychology*, **57**(3), 349–57.

Wykes, T. (ed.) (1994) *Violence and the Health Care Professions*, Chapman & Hall, London.

Yalom, I.D. (1989) *Love's Executioner and Other Tales of Psychotherapy*, Penguin, Harmondsworth, UK.

Zilbergeld, B. (1983) *The Shrinking of America: Myths of Psychological Change*, Little, Boston, MA.

Appendix: Addresses of some UK and US counselling journals

Bereavement Care Journal
CRUSE, 126 Sheen Road,
Richmond, Surrey TW9 1UR, UK.

British Journal of Guidance and Counselling and
Counselling Psychology Quarterly
Carfax Publishing Company,
PO Box 25, Abingdon, Oxford-shire OX14 3UE, UK.

British Journal of Psychotherapy
Artesian Books Ltd,
18 Artesian Road,
London W2 5AR, UK;

Changes
Journals Department, Afterhurst Limited, 27 Church Road, Hove, East Sussex BN3 2FA, UK.

Counselling
BAC, 1 Regent Place, Rugby, Warwickshire CV21 2PJ, UK.

Counselling Psychologist
Sage Publications, 28 Banner Street, London EC1Y 8QE, UK; 2455 Teller Road, Newbury Park, CA 91320, USA

Counselling Psychology Review
BPS, St Andrews House,
Leicester LE1 7DR, UK.

Journal of Counseling & Development
American Counseling Association, 5999 Stevenson Alexandria, VA 22304–3300, USA.

Journal of Psychotherapy Integration
Plenum Publishing Corporation, 233 Spring Street, New York, NY 10013, USA; British Institute of Integrative Psychotherapy, 10 Parkmead, London SW15 5BS, UK.

The Therapist
ETSI, The Office, 7 Chapel Road, Worthing, West Sussex BN11 1EG, UK.

Journal of Counseling Psychology
American Psychological Association, 750 First Street NE, Washington DC 20002–4242, USA

Name index